Contents

Key to pronunciations

The pronunciation of a word, when necessary, is given by respelling it, and it is shown between forward slashes (e.g. '**Adult** is usually pronounced /**ad**-ult/ in British English'). This system is very easy to follow, but a few symbols need explanation:

a	the vowel sound in 'cat'
I	the sound of the word 'eye'
i	the vowel sound in 'kid'
oo	the vowel sound in 'root'
ow	the vowel sound in 'cow'
th	the 'hard th' in 'thick'
th	the 'soft th' in 'this'
uu	the vowel sound in 'book'
uh	the sound of the 'a' in 'along'
'	a hint of an /uh/ sound, as in /**foh**-k'l/ 'focal'

Preface

The *Oxford A-Z of English Usage* offers straightforward, up-to-date guidance on questions of English usage, some very familiar to many readers, some probably not so familiar, but all affecting the language we choose and how effectively we get our message across.

The advice and information given are based on analysis of the Oxford English Corpus, a database containing more than two billion words of real 21st-century English, collected from a huge variety of sources. The entries therefore reflect modern practice and attitudes, revealing, for example, how *straight-laced* is now actually used more commonly than the traditional spelling *strait-laced*. The entries are also illustrated with examples of real English drawn from the Corpus.

Common confusions such as *uninterested* and *disinterested* are explained, differences between British and American practice are highlighted, and a realistic attitude is taken towards famous examples such as splitting infinitives, ending a sentence with a preposition, and when it is correct to say *you and me* or *you and I*.

Longer articles allow discussion of wider points, such as the dramatic changes that have occurred in English in recent years through attempts to use 'gender-neutral' language, and why it is important to use hyphens correctly in some contexts, while it makes little difference whether many compounds are written with a hyphen or not.

Thanks to Oxford's unique resources, this book simultaneously reflects real, modern English usage and makes use of the expertise and authority for which Oxford Dictionaries are world-famous. To explore the language further try Oxford Dictionaries Online. This free site is updated regularly and allows you to search the *Oxford Dictionary of English* and its US counterpart, the *New Oxford American Dictionary*. It also offers information on usage, grammar, and writing, Word of the Day, and a language blog. The subscription-based Oxford Dictionaries Pro features linked, fully searchable dictionaries and thesauruses, audio pronunciations, millions of example sentences, and specialist language reference resources. Find Oxford Dictionaries Online at www.oxforddictionaries.com.

a, an

A and **an** are the two forms of 'the indefinite article'. See AN for information on which to use before

- words beginning with **h**, e.g. *hotel*
- words beginning with a letter that is normally a vowel, e.g. *unique*
- initialisms, e.g. *SAS*

abbreviations

People are often unsure about these questions to do with abbreviations:

- whether to write them with capital letters
- which ones need full stops
- when to use apostrophes

There are four main kinds of abbreviation: shortenings, contractions, initialisms, and acronyms. Standard practice depends on the kind of abbreviation in question.

1 Shortenings are abbreviations where the beginning or end of the word has been dropped: *cello* = violoncello, *flu* = influenza, *ad* = advertisement, *bike* = bicycle, *pub* = public house, *rhino* = rhinoceros, *telly* = television. In some cases the longer form is only used in technical or formal writing and could sound quaint or affected in speech.

- Because such shortenings are now an accepted part of the language, you no longer need to put an apostrophe at the beginning or end.
- Where the shortening is only ever written, such as *Dec.* = December, *Tue.* = Tuesday, or *etc.* = et cetera, a full stop is used.

2 Contractions are a type of abbreviation in which letters from the middle of the word are omitted: *Dr* = Doctor, *St* = Saint, *Ltd* = Limited.

▶

- Because the last letter of the word is present, no full stop is used: *Dr*, *Revd*, *Mrs*.
- In verb forms and archaic words, the omitted letters are replaced by an apostrophe: *can't* = cannot, *we've* = we have; *ne'er-do-well* = never-do-well, *o'er* = over.

3 **Initialisms** are abbreviations which consist of the initial letters of words and which are pronounced as separate letters: *a.m., BBC, MOD, MP, QC, UN, TUC*.

- British style is not to include full stops, whereas American style tends to.
- The plural is formed by adding an **-s**, now normally without an apostrophe (e.g. *MPs* and *QCs* rather than *MP's* or *QC's*). Possessives are formed in the usual way (e.g. *an MP's salary*; *several MPs' secretaries*).

4 **Acronyms** are words formed from the initial letters of other words, and pronounced as they are spelled: *Aids*, *NATO*. Some of them, such as *radar* and *laser*, have become normal words.

- They can be written all as capitals or only with an initial capital, and house styles vary. With some words, such as *Aids*, there is a tendency to have only an initial capital.

able-bodied, abled

It is best to avoid using **able-bodied** to mean 'not having a physical disability', since many people with disabilities object to its use in this way. Their preferred word is **non-disabled**. **Abled**, meaning 'not disabled', is a revival of an obsolete 16th-century word, and has been recorded in print in the US since the 1980s. It is now used in the phrase **differently abled** as a more positive alternative to **disabled**.

Aboriginal, Aborigine

Australian **Aborigines** prefer to be known as **Indigenous Australians**, and this phrase is becoming more and more standard. While both **Aboriginal** and **Aborigine** may be used as nouns, **Aborigine** is the commoner and preferred choice. **Aboriginal** is the term used by the Australian government, but is disliked by **Indigenous Australians** themselves.

abstruse

For the confusion between **abstruse** and **obtuse**, see OBTUSE.

access

The verb **to access** is standard and common in computing and related terminology. But its use outside computing contexts, although well established, is sometimes criticized as being 'jargon': *you must use a password to access the account*. If you want an alternative, you could use a word or phrase such as 'enter' or 'gain access to': *to gain access to the information*. For more information on formations of this kind, see VERBS FORMED FROM NOUNS.

accusative, accusatory

Accusative is a grammatical term referring to the grammatical case of the object of a verb. Using it to mean 'accusing', as in *an accusative tone*, is incorrect. The correct word is **accusatory**: *turning on his heel, he pointed an accusatory finger at von Laffeyhosen*.

acknowledgement

The spelling with **-dge-** is more common in all varieties of English than the spelling with **-dg-**, though both are correct. British English tends to prefer the form with **-dge-**.

AD

AD is normally written in small capital letters and should be placed before the numerals, as in AD *375* (not *375* AD). This is because AD is an abbreviation of *anno domini*, which means 'in the year of our Lord', and should logically come before the year. However, it is normal to write *the third century*

AD (not AD *the third century*). AD is written without full stops after the letters. See also BC.

addenda, addendum

Addenda is a Latin plural form meaning 'a list of additional items'. If there is only one item, **addendum** is the correct traditional form to use. **Addenda** should therefore only ever be used as a plural, not as a singular. So, you may well be thought wrong if you use **addenda** as a singular, as in *a new edition with an invaluable addenda*, instead of the correct *a new edition with invaluable addenda*. Worse still is to use the non-existent plural *addendas*. See also LATIN PLURALS.

address

The verb **address**, although it seems at first glance to promise forceful action, can justifiably be criticized for being overused. Moreover, when someone undertakes to *address an issue* it is often unclear to what exactly they are committing. Will they merely note it as something to be dealt with at an unspecified future date, analyse it in depth, or actually resolve it as soon as humanly possible? To avoid what some people regard as a bit of a woolly cliché, it may be better to specify the exact measures you intend taking. Or else use **resolve**, **deal with**, or **sort out** instead.

admission, admittance

Admission traditionally referred to the price paid for entry or the right to enter: *admission was £5*. **Admittance** more often referred to physical entry: *we were denied admittance by a large man with a forbidding scowl*. In this meaning of 'permission or right to enter', these words have become almost interchangeable, although **admittance** is more formal and technical.

ad nauseam

The correct spelling of this Latin phrase is with **-eam** at the end. Some people write it with **-eum**, perhaps influenced by the fact that the phrase *ad infinitum* ends in **-um**. Whatever the reason for the mistake, if you go to the trouble of using a Latin phrase in the first place, it is best to write it correctly.

adult

The standard way to pronounce **adult** in British English is to emphasize the first syllable: /**ad**-ult/. Emphasizing the second syllable, /uh-**dult**/, is an alternative, and is the standard for speakers of American English. This pronunciation is becoming more widespread in British English, and, though many people dislike it, is acceptable. Interestingly, in 1884 the *Oxford English Dictionary* suggested the second pronunciation as the preferred version.

adversary

The standard way to pronounce **adversary** in British English is to emphasize the first syllable only: /**ad**-ver-suh-ree/. Speakers of American English add a secondary stress before the third syllable, which they also pronounce differently: /**ad**-ver-**sai**-ree/.

adverse

Adverse and **averse** are related in origin but mean different things. **Adverse** means 'unfavourable or harmful' and is normally used of conditions and effects rather than people, as in *adverse weather conditions*. **Averse**, on the other hand, is used of people (nearly always followed by **to**), and means 'having a strong dislike or opposition to something', as in *I am not averse to helping out*. A common mistake is to use **adverse** instead of **averse**, as in *he is not adverse to making a profit*.

advertise

Advertise is correctly spelled *-ise*, never *-ize*.

adviser, advisor

The spelling **advisor** is about half as common as **adviser**. More common in North America than in Britain, it is a more recent development and is still regarded by some people as incorrect.

a

affect

Affect and **effect** are quite different in meaning, though frequently confused. **Affect** is primarily a verb meaning 'make a difference to', as in *their gender need not affect their career*. **Effect**, on the other hand, is used both as a noun and a verb, meaning 'a result' as a noun (*move the cursor until you get the effect you want*) or 'to bring about a result' as a verb (*growth in the economy can only be effected by stringent economic controls*). The two verbs have very similar meanings, so it often pays to think carefully which one you want.

African American, Afro-American

African American is the currently accepted term in the US for Americans of African origin, having first become prominent in the late 1980s. it has largely replaced **Afro-American**, which was first recorded in the 19th century and became widespread in the 1960s and 1970s. In Britain, **black** is the standard term.

afterward, afterwards

Afterward is a standard form only in US English, but it is still outnumbered two to one by **afterwards** in the American writing in the Oxford English Corpus. In all other varieties of English, **afterwards** is the only customary form.

agenda

Though **agenda** is the plural of **agendum** in Latin, in standard modern English it is normally used as a singular noun. It therefore has a standard English plural form: **agendas**, not '*agendae*', as is sometimes seen.

aggravate

Aggravate in the sense 'to annoy or exasperate' dates back to the 17th century and has been so used by respected writers ever since. This use is still regarded as incorrect by some traditionalists on the grounds that it is too radical a departure from the etymological meaning of 'to make heavy'. It is, however, comparable to meaning changes in hundreds of other words which have long been accepted without comment.

ago

When **ago** is followed by a clause, the clause should be introduced by **that** rather than **since**, e.g. *it was sixty years ago that I left this place*, but you could avoid **ago** by writing *it is sixty years since I left this place*.

agreement

Agreement (also called *concord*) is the correct relation of different parts of a sentence to each other: for example, the form of a verb should correspond to its subject: *the **house was** small, and its **walls were** painted white*; again, the gender and number (singular or plural) of a pronoun should conform to those of the person or thing it refers to: *he had never been close enough to a **girl** to consider making **her** his wife*. As English has lost many inflections over centuries of use, problems of agreement only arise in the two cases just mentioned. This article deals with noun-verb agreement. Discussion of pronoun agreement and other aspects of verb agreement is dealt with under individual entries: see AND, ANY, AS WELL AS, EACH, EITHER, GENDER-NEUTRAL LANGUAGE, HALF, KIND, NONE, NUMBER, OR, SORT, and THEY. Here are some typical difficulties that people have in making verbs agree with noun subjects.

1 Sentences, especially long ones, in which the verb is separated from its singular subject by intervening words in the plural can make the speaker or writer put the verb in the plural, but these examples are incorrect: *the **consequence** of long periods of inactivity or situations in which patients cannot look after themselves **are** often quite severe and long-lasting*; ***copyright** of Vivienne's papers **are** in the keeping of the Haigh-Wood family*.
In the first example there are three options: ▶

change *consequence* to *consequences*, change *are* to *is*, or (probably best) recast the sentence more simply, *e.g. Long periods of inactivity... can often have quite severe and long-lasting consequences.*

2 Two nouns joined by **and**: these normally form a plural subject and require a plural verb: *speed and accuracy are what is needed*; *fish and chips are served in the evening.* But when the noun phrase is regarded as a singular unit, it can take a singular verb: *fish and chips is my favourite meal*; *wine, women, and song was the leitmotiv of his lifestyle.* This can extend to concepts that are distinct in themselves but are regarded as a single item in a particular sentence: *a certain cynicism and resignation comes along with advancing years.*

The last convention is very old, with evidence dating back to Old and Middle English. Clearly there will be borderline cases, and then it is what sounds natural that matters: ***the hurt and disbelief** of parents' friends and families **is/are** already quite real.*

3 Two or more nouns can be joined by words other than **and**, e.g. *accompanied by*, *as well as*, *not to mention*, *together with*, etc. These noun groups are followed by a singular verb if the first noun or noun phrase is singular, because the addition is not regarded as part of the grammatical subject: *even such a very profitable company, along with many other companies in the UK, **is** not prepared to pay even a reasonable amount*; *Daddy had on the hairy tweed **jacket** with leather elbow patches which, together with his pipe, **was** his trademark.*

4 When a subject and a complement of different number (singular/plural) are separated by the verb *to be* (or verbs such as *become*, *seem*, etc.), the verb should agree with the number of the subject, not that of the complement:

- (singular subject and plural complement) *the only **traffic** **is** ox-carts and bicycles*; *the **view** it obscured **was** pipes, fire escapes, and a sooty wall* ▶

- (plural subject and singular complement) *the **socials were** a big deal to her; the March **events were** a natural stage in the evolution of democracy in the country.*

  NB: There are some exceptions, depending on the meaning in particular cases: *more **nurses*** (i.e. the topic of more nurses) ***is** the next item on the agenda.*

albeit

1 **Albeit** is not an archaic word, although it may sound like one. It is used as a conjunction with the meaning 'though', to make a contrast with or to modify a preceding expression: *it is an unwelcome, albeit necessary, piece of legislation.*

2 It should not be written as the three words 'all be it' in modern Standard English.

3 Even though most conjunctions are used with verbs, e.g. *you just keep going because you have no choice*, it is not good style to use **albeit** with a verb, as in *Mr Gaunt is as culpable as the others, albeit he was not involved in any of the incidents*. The explanation for this is that **albeit** derived from the phrase 'all be it that', which already contained a verb.

alibi

The word **alibi**, which in Latin means 'elsewhere', has been used since the 18th century to mean 'an assertion by a person that he or she was elsewhere'. In the 20th century a new meaning arose, originally in the US, of 'an excuse'. This is a fairly common and natural extension of the core meaning, but, though widely accepted in standard English, it is still regarded as incorrect by some people.

alright

There is no logical reason for insisting that **alright** is incorrect and should always be written as **all right**, when other single-word forms such as **altogether** have long been accepted. The fact that **alright** is not recorded until the end of the

19th century, while other similar merged spellings such as **altogether** and **already** date from much earlier, is no reason for denouncing it, but many people still find it unacceptable in formal writing.

alternative

The adjective **alternate** is sometimes used in place of **alternative**, especially in American English. In British English the two words continue to be quite distinct: **alternative** means 'available as another possibility or choice', as in *some European countries follow an alternative approach*. **Alternate** means 'every other', as in *they meet on alternate Sundays*, or 'each following the other in a regular pattern', as in *alternate layers of potato and sauce*. The use of **alternate** to mean **alternative**, as in *we will need to find alternate sources of fuel*, is common in North America, and many US dictionaries now record it as equivalent in this meaning to **alternative**. In British English, however, it is not yet considered good style.

although

The form **although** can be replaced by **though**, the only difference being that **although** tends to be more formal than **though**.

altogether

Note that **altogether** and **all together** do not mean the same thing. **Altogether** means 'in total', as in *there are six bedrooms altogether*, whereas **all together** means 'all in one place' or 'all at once', as in *it was good to have a group of friends all together; they came in all together*.

alumnus

Alumnus comes from Latin, and refers to an ex-student of a particular university or similar educational establishment. The plural is **alumni**. The technically correct form for a female ex-student is **alumna**, the plural of which is **alumnae**. **Alumni** is the form to use when referring to groups including both sexes, and **alumnae** when they are exclusively female. Although

alumnus is a masculine noun in Latin, it is sometimes used to refer to a female ex-student in contexts where the feminine form might sound overacademic: *she's touted as the number one alumnus of Southern Methodist University*. **Alumnus** is pronounced /uh-**lum**-nuhs/. **Alumni** is generally pronounced as /uh-**lum**-nI/, and **alumnae** as /uh-**lum**-nee/.

Alzheimer's disease

This condition is often incorrectly spelled with a letter **t** inserted before the **z**, reflecting its pronunciation. Some German names used in English expressions do contain **tz**, such as *Hertz* and *Helmholtz*, but **z** in **Alzheimer's** is pronounced /-ts-/ anyway: /**alts**-hI-muhz/.

a.m.

As an abbreviation of Latin **ante meridiem**, meaning 'before noon', **a.m.** is pronounced as two letters and written with two full stops in the form **8.15 a.m.** (in American English **8:15 a.m.**). Note that **12.00 a.m.** is midnight and **12.00 p.m.** is midday, but because of the uncertainty these designations cause, the explicit forms **12 midnight** and **12 noon** or **12 midday** are clearer. The abbreviation is sometimes used informally as a noun: *I arrived here this a.m.*, but this use is not acceptable in any kind of formal writing.

American Indian

The term **American Indian** has been steadily replaced in the US, especially in official contexts, by the more recent term **Native American** (first recorded in the 1950s and becoming prominent in the 1970s). Some people prefer **Native American** as being a more accurate and respectful description as well as avoiding the stereotype of cowboys and Indians in the stories of the Wild West. **American Indian** is still widespread in general use even in the US, however, perhaps at least partly because it is not normally regarded as offensive by American Indians themselves. Nevertheless, since the category **American Indian** is very broad, it is preferable, where possible, to name the specific people, e.g. **Apache**, **Comanche**, or **Sioux**.

amount

It is always correct to use **amount** with nouns with a singular meaning, such as *money*, *time*, and *energy*. With nouns which have a plural form or meaning, it is always right to use **number**: *the number of people*, *the number of patients*, *the number of accidents*, etc. But quite often people use **amount** instead of **number** with plural nouns, as in *the amount of nutrients available*; *the amount of bribes*; *the amount of calls at night*. This use has a long tradition and is broadly forgivable in speech, but it is best avoided in writing: people with tidy grammatical minds may be as irritated by it as they are by the use of *less* when *fewer* is correct, as in *customers with less than five items*.

an

Opinions differ over whether to use **a** or **an** before certain words beginning with **h-** when the first syllable is unstressed: *a historical document* or *an historical document*; *a hotel* or *an hotel*. The uncertainty arises for historical reasons: **an** was common in the 18th and 19th centuries, because the initial **h** was often not pronounced in these words. Nowadays, use of **a** or **an** varies in both writing and speaking. Only older speakers are likely to pronounce words such as **hotel** and **historic** with the silent **h**; nevertheless, *an hotel* and *an historic event* are often heard and are equally correct.

In writing, there are many examples in the Oxford English Corpus of **an** being used with **habitual**, **historian**, **historic(al)**, **horrendous**, and **horrific**, albeit less often than **a**. Remember that whether you use **a** or **an** depends on the sound at the start of the following word, however it is spelled. For instance, although the letter **u** normally represents a vowel, the words **unique** and **uniform** start with a **y** sound, which is a consonant, and it is therefore correct to write and say *a unique feature* and *a uniform approach*. This also applies to abbreviations where the initials are pronounced as the names of letters, such as *EU* and *SAS*. The names of the letters **E** and **S** are said as /ee/ (a vowel sound) and /ess/ (also starting with a vowel sound), so you would say and write both *an EU ruling* and *an SAS unit*.

analogous

Strictly speaking, **analogous** should not be used merely as a supposedly stylish synonym for *similar*. It means 'comparable in certain respects', especially where the analogy makes the nature of the things compared clearer: *they saw the relationship between a ruler and his subjects as analogous to that of father and children*. As in the example just shown, the preposition to use with **analogous** is **to**, rather than **with**.
Analogous is pronounced with a hard **g**.

and

1 Many people believe that conjunctions such as **and**, **but**, and **because** should not be used to start a sentence. They argue that a sentence starting with a conjunction expresses an incomplete thought and is therefore incorrect. Writers down the centuries, from Shakespeare to David Lodge, have ignored this advice, however, typically for rhetorical effect: *What are the government's chances of winning in court? And what are the consequences?*

2 For the expression **try and do something**, see TRY AND.

3 For information about whether it is more correct to say *both the boys and the girls* or *both the boys and girls*, see BOTH.

4 Where items in a list are separated by **and**, the following verb needs to be in the plural: see OR.

antidisestablishmentarianism

Antidisestablishmentarianism is almost never found in genuine use and is most often merely cited as an example of a very long word. Other similar curiosities are *floccinaucinihilipilification* and *pneumonoultramicroscopicsilicovolcanoconiosis*, the second being generally reckoned to be the longest word in any dictionary. The longest word to be encountered in Britain is the Welsh place name

a

Llanfairpwllgwyngyllgogerychwyrndrobwllllantysiliogogogoch, which is generally abbreviated to Llanfair PG; this name was created in the 19th century.

antisocial

On the difference in use between **antisocial**, **unsocial**, and **unsociable**, see UNSOCIABLE.

anxious

Anxious and **eager** both mean 'looking forward to something', but they have different overtones. **Eager** suggests enthusiasm about something and a positive outlook: *I'm eager to get started on my vacation*. **Anxious** implies worry about something: *I'm anxious to get started before it rains*. This is a useful distinction to maintain.

any

When used as a pronoun, **any** can be used with either a singular or a plural verb, depending on the context. If **any** refers to a singular uncountable noun, the verb is always singular: *we needed more sugar but there* ***wasn't any*** *left*. Uncertainty occasionally arises, however, when the noun referred to is plural, especially in questions and hypotheses: ***are any*** *of the above suitable? if* ***any*** *of them* ***escape****, notify the police*. The general tendency is to use the verb in the plural, especially in conversation. If you use the verb in the singular, you are presupposing that only one person or thing is being referred to, as in *if* ***any*** *of them* ***inspires*** *the public* ... Otherwise, use with a singular verb is likely these days to sound stilted or affected.

See also AGREEMENT.

anyone

The one-word form **anyone** is not the same as the two-word form **any one**, and the two forms cannot be used interchangeably. **Anyone** means 'any person or people', as in *anyone who wants to can attend*. **Any one** means 'any single (person or thing)', as in *no more than twelve new members are admitted in any one year*.

apostrophe

This insignificant-looking mark is the loose cannon of the punctuation world, responsible for more howlers than any other punctuation mark. So, it may be helpful to refresh your memory about its two very distinct functions. It is also useful to be on the lookout for the obvious traps apostrophes can lay for you, as explained under **four pitfalls to avoid**, below.

- Apostrophes stand for letters that have been missed out.
- They show that someone or something owns something.

1 Missed out letters

In speaking we often leave out sounds from certain words, particularly verbs: we tend to say *I'm going*, not *I am going*. In other cases, we run two words together: *I* ***shan't*** *go* instead of *I shall not go*.
The apostrophe shows where we have left out these sounds:
won't = will not
can't = cannot
she's = she is; she has
you're = you are
In a few other words, often rather old-fashioned or poetic ones, apostrophes also show letters missed out: *o'er* (= over); *ne'er-do-well*; *rock 'n' roll*.

2 Ownership

- The apostrophe indicates that someone owns something, or shows a relationship between the things mentioned:
Jack's new mountain bike
the parrot's cage
the book's cover
- To help you decide if the apostrophe comes before or after the letter **s**, first try rephrasing your sentence using the word **of**. Then look carefully at the final ▶

letter of the relevant word as it now appears. The correct place to put the apostrophe is immediately after that letter. For example *in a week's time* becomes *in the time of a week*, which shows that the apostrophe goes after the letter **k**. But *in three weeks' time* becomes *in the time of three weeks*, proving that the apostrophe should come after the letter **s**.

3 Four pitfalls to avoid

- Never use an apostrophe to show the plural of a word when there is no ownership involved. You will often see this mistake on shop signs or on grocers' stalls: *apple's and pear's*, which should be *apples and pears*. The same rule applies to plurals which are abbreviations: *MPs, QCs, DVDs*. See also the entry for 's.
- Remember the difference between **it's** and **its**. The first one shows that a letter has been left out: *it's on the trolley*. The second indicates ownership, but in spite of that has no apostrophe: *the kitten licked its paws*. **Its** in this meaning is the same type of word as *ours, yours, his*, and *hers*, where it is clear that no apostrophe is required.
- **Who's** and **whose** are often confused. Remember those corny old jokes that go *Knock, knock!—Who's there*? In that case, ***who's*** is obviously short for *who is*. **Whose** is like **its**: although it shows ownership, it needs no apostrophe: *that's the man* ***whose*** *son got married to my cousin*.
- **You're** and **your** are very easy to muddle up when writing at speed. The first indicates a missing letter: *you're late again* = you are late again. The second is like **its** and **whose**—ownership, but no apostrophe: *is this* ***your*** *wallet, Bob*?

a

appendix

Appendix has the plural form **appendices** when referring to parts of books and documents, and **appendixes** when referring to the bodily organ. For more information on the plural of Latin words, see LATIN PLURALS.

appraise, apprise

The verb **appraise** is frequently confused with **apprise**. **Appraise** means 'to assess', as in *a need to appraise existing techniques*, or 'to value', as in *have the gold watch appraised by an expert*. **Apprise** means 'to inform' and is often used in the construction **apprise someone of something**, as in *psychiatrists were apprised of his condition*. People often incorrectly use **appraise** rather than **apprise**, as in *once appraised of the real facts, there was only one person who showed any opposition*.

aristocrat, aristocratic

There are two ways of pronouncing **aristocrat**. You can emphasize either the first syllable (/**a**-ris-tuh-krat/) or the second (/a-**ris**-tuh-krat/). The first pronunciation is still the standard one in British English. The second is the standard American pronunciation, but is fast gaining ground in Britain too, particularly among transatlantic academics and pundits. Interestingly, it was once the standard in Britain, so it could be seen as a revival rather than an intrusion. **Aristocratic** is normally pronounced emphasizing the fourth syllable in British English (/a-ris-tuh-**kra**-tik/) and emphasizing the second in American English (/a-**ris**-tuh-kra-tik/).

around

1 On the difference in use between **round** and **around**, see ROUND.

2 It is curious how some words become so popular that they oust the ones people routinely used before. **Around** is such a word. It is now, arguably, overused as an all-purpose preposition, generally to show the relationship between two abstract ideas: *I think there's a misconception around that, somehow; we would*

like some flexibility around that implementation; there are concerns around the following issues. *While there is no objection in principle to using **around** in the ways shown, it comes laden with the heavy baggage of bureaucracy or of the caring professions. It seems to have expanded from its core use in the common phrase **issues around**, through similar contexts to general use, willy-nilly. Prepositions such as **over** and **about** could replace it in all the examples above with absolutely no loss of meaning, and with a considerable gain in freshness or sincerity.*

artefact

Artefact, 'a product of human art or workmanship' comes from the Latin *arte factum*, 'made by art'. The spelling with the letter **e** is much the more common in British English. In American English, **artifact**, corresponding to pronunciation rather than etymology, is the preferred form, but would be looked on unfavourably in most of the circles in Britain in which such a word would be used.

as

1 For a discussion of whether it is correct to say:
he's not as shy as I rather than *he's not as shy as me*
or
I live in the same street as she rather than *I live in the same street as her*
see PERSONAL PRONOUN.

2 For more information on when **as** is preferable to **like**, see LIKE.

ascribe

Ascribe and **subscribe** are sometimes confused. If you **ascribe** a quality **to** a person or group of people, you think it is typical of them, as in *tough-mindedness is a quality commonly ascribed to top bosses*. If you **subscribe to** a belief, view, or idea, you agree with it: *we prefer to subscribe to an alternative explanation*. It is wrong to give this meaning to **ascribe to**, as in *which theory do you ascribe to?*

as far as

Using **as far as** to specify something, as in the phrase, *as far as the money, you can forget it*, is well established in American usage and is a useful shorthand for the older **as far as . . . is/are concerned**. Nevertheless, many more conservative British speakers are likely to object to it, so it is best avoided with a British audience.

Asian

In Britain, **Asian** is used to refer to people who come from (or whose parents came from) the Indian subcontinent, but in North America it is used to refer to people from the Far East.

Asiatic

The standard and accepted term when referring to individual people is **Asian** rather than **Asiatic**, which can be offensive. However, **Asiatic** is standard in scientific and technical use, for example in biological and anthropological classifications.

assurance

In life insurance, a technical distinction is made between **assurance** and **insurance**. **Assurance** is used of policies under whose terms a payment is guaranteed, either after a fixed term or on the death of the insured person; **insurance** is the general word, and is used in particular of policies under whose terms a payment would be made only in certain circumstances (e.g. accident or death within a limited period).

asterisk

Asterisk should be pronounced with an /**-isk**/ sound at the end, to match the spelling, and not as though it were spelled **-ix**. **Asterix** is a character in a cartoon strip.

as well as

A verb following **as well as** should be singular if the noun or pronoun that precedes **as well as** is singular: *their* ***singing*** *as well as acting* **is** *exemplary*. This is because the addition (here, the phrase *as well as acting*) is regarded as an aside and not as part of the main sentence. This is in contrast to what would happen if **as well as** were replaced by **and**. For more information see AND and OR.

aural

The words **aural** ('relating to the ears or the sense of hearing') and **oral** ('spoken rather than written') are both pronounced as /**aw**-ruhl/ in Received Pronunciation, which is sometimes a source of confusion. However, although a distinctive pronunciation for **aural** has been proposed, namely /**ow**-ruhl/, it is very little used.

Australoid

The term **Australoid** belongs to a set of terms introduced by 19th-century anthropologists attempting to categorize human races. Such terms are associated with outdated notions of racial types, and so are now potentially offensive and best avoided. See MONGOLOID.

author

Some people object to the verb **author** as in *she has authored several books on wildlife*. It is well established, though, especially in North America. See also VERBS FORMED FROM NOUNS.

averse

On the confusion of **averse** and **adverse**, see ADVERSE.

awhile

The adverb **awhile** as in *we paused awhile* should be written as one word. The noun phrase, meaning 'a period of time', should be written as two words, especially when preceded by a preposition: *Margaret rested for a while*; *we'll be there in a while*.

backward

1 In their adverbial uses **backward** and **backwards** are interchangeable in meaning: *the car rolled slowly backward* and *the car rolled slowly backwards*. **Backward** is mainly used in

US English, but even there **backwards** is more common, as the Oxford English Corpus reveals. As an adjective, on the other hand, the standard form is **backward** rather than **backwards**: uses such as *a backwards glance* would generally be considered incorrect.

2 To describe a person with learning difficulties as **backward** is nowadays offensive.

bacterium

Bacteria is the plural form, from Latin, of **bacterium**. Like any other plural it should be used with the plural form of the verb: *the **bacteria** causing salmonella **are** killed by thorough cooking*, not *the **bacteria** causing salmonella **is** killed by thorough cooking*. However, general unfamiliarity with the form **bacterium** means that **bacteria** is often mistakenly treated as a singular form, as in the second example above. For other examples of this kind of mistake, see NOUNS, SINGULAR AND PLURAL.

balk, baulk

However this verb is spelled, it is usually pronounced so that you can hear the letter **l** (/bawlk/). Some older British speakers may pronounce it without the **l**. The spelling without **u** is now the more common one in all varieties of English.

Bantu

The word **Bantu** became a strongly offensive term under the old apartheid regime in South Africa, especially when used to refer to a single individual. In standard current use in South Africa the term **black** or **African** is used as a collective or non-specific word for African peoples. The term **Bantu** has, however, continued to be accepted as a neutral 'scientific' term outside South Africa to refer to the group of languages and their speakers collectively.

barbecue

Barbecue is often spelled **barbeque**. It is easy to see that this is because of how the word is pronounced and because of the informal abbreviations **BBQ** and **Bar-B-Q**. The spelling **barbeque** is now accepted in standard English.

barely

Barely, like **scarcely**, should normally be followed by *when*, not *than*, to introduce a subsequent clause: *he had barely reached the door when he collapsed*.

basis

It is very common for **basis** to be included in phrases describing how often something happens: *on a daily basis*, *on a weekly basis*, and so forth. Unless the word is really required in a technical context, e.g. *inspection of the facility is carried out on the basis of a weekly rota*, ordinary time adverbs such as **weekly** or **daily**, or a phrase such as **every week** can easily and more economically be used instead: *I do it weekly*.

bated breath

It is a common mistake to write **baited breath** instead of **bated breath**. The first written example of the original phrase is in Shakespeare's *The Merchant of Venice*, and **bate** is a shortened version of **abate**. About a third of all examples of this phrase in the Oxford English Corpus are with the incorrect spelling.

For more information, see FOLK ETYMOLOGY.

baulk

See BALK.

BC

BC is normally printed in small capitals and placed *after* the year, as in *72* BC or *the 2nd century* BC. This position is logical since BC stands for 'before Christ'; compare with AD. It is not written with full stops after each letter.

bear

Until the 18th century **borne** and **born** were simply variants of the past participle of **bear**, used interchangeably with no distinction in meaning. By around 1775, however, the present distinction in use had become established. **Borne** became the standard past participle for the transitive verb: *she has borne you* *another son*; *the findings have been borne out*. **Born** became the standard, neutral way to refer to birth: *she was born in 1965*; *he was born lucky*; *I was born and bred in Gloucester*. The most common mistake is to write **born** instead of **borne**, as in the incorrect *his suspicions have not been born out*.

because

1 When **because** follows a negative construction the meaning can be ambiguous. In the sentence *he did not go because he was ill*, for example, it is not clear whether it means 'the reason he did not go was that he was ill' or 'being ill was not the reason for him going; there was another reason'. Some usage guides recommend using a comma for the first interpretation (*he did not go, because he was ill*) and no comma for the second interpretation, but it is probably wiser to avoid using **because** after a negative altogether; one way would be to turn the sentence around: *because he was ill, he didn't go*.

2 As with other conjunctions such as **but** and **and**, it is still widely held that it is incorrect to begin a sentence with **because**. It has, however, long been used in this way in both written and spoken English (typically for rhetorical effect), and is quite acceptable.

3 On the construction **the reason . . . is because**, see REASON.

beg

The original meaning of the phrase **beg the question** belongs to the field of logic and is a translation of Latin *petitio principii*, literally meaning 'laying claim to a principle', i.e. assuming something that ought to be proved first, as in the following sentence: *by devoting such a large budget to Civics, we are begging the question of its usefulness*. For some people this is still the only correct meaning. However, over the last 100 years or so another, more general use has arisen: 'invite an obvious question', as in *some definitions of mental illness beg the question of what constitutes normal behaviour*. This is by far the commoner use today and is widely accepted in modern standard English.

b

behalf

Behalf is used in the phrase **on behalf of** and the rare variant **in behalf of**, the second used in American English. It can mean either 'in the interests of', as in *he campaigned on behalf of the poor*, or 'as a representative of', as in *I attended on her behalf*. It is increasingly being used to express responsibility for something, as in *this was a mistake on behalf of the government*, where **on the part of** is the appropriate phrase. This use is generally considered incorrect and should be avoided in writing.

beholden, behove

If you are **beholden** to someone for something, you owe them something in return for favours or services that they have done you: *politicians who are beholden to big business*. In formal language, if **it behoves you** to do something, it is your responsibility or duty to do it: *it behoves the House to assure itself that there is no conceivable alternative*. The form 'behoven' created by combining the two words is occasionally used instead of **beholden** but is not yet acceptable in standard English.

beside, besides

1 Both **beside** and **besides** have the meaning of 'apart from'. Some people claim that only **besides** should be used in this meaning: *he commissioned work from other artists besides Minton* rather than *he commissioned work from other artists beside Minton*. Although there is little logical basis for such a view, in standard English it can be clearer to use **besides** in this meaning, because **beside** can be ambiguous: *beside the cold meat, there are platters of trout and salmon* could mean either 'the cold meat is next to the trout and salmon' or 'apart from the cold meat, there are also trout and salmon'.

2 **Besides** is the correct form to use as an adverb meaning 'as well', as in *I'm capable of doing the work, and a lot more besides* or *besides, I wasn't sure*.

best

See WELL.

better

In the verb phrase **had better do something** the word **had** acts as an auxiliary verb and in informal spoken contexts is often dropped, as in *you better not come tonight*. In writing, the **had** may be contracted to **'d**, but it should not be dropped altogether.

between

In standard English it is correct to say *between you and me* but incorrect to say *between you and I*. There is a very good reason for this. A preposition such as **between** is correctly followed by object pronouns such as *me*, *him*, *her*, and *us* rather than subject pronouns such as *I*, *he*, *she*, and *we*. It is therefore correct to say *between us* or *between him and her* and it is clearly incorrect to say *between we* or *between he and she*.

People mistakenly say *between you and I* through confusing what follows a preposition and what ordinarily comes at the beginning of a sentence. They know that it is not correct to say *John and me went to the shops* and that the correct sentence is *John and I went to the shops*. They therefore assume that 'and me' should be replaced by 'and I' in all cases. For more information see PERSONAL PRONOUN.

bi-

1 The meaning of **bimonthly** and other similar words such as **biweekly** and **biyearly** is ambiguous. Such words can either mean 'occurring twice a month/week/year' or 'occurring every two months/weeks/years'. The only way to avoid this ambiguity is to use alternative expressions like 'every two months' and 'twice a month'.

2 **Biennial** means 'taking place every two years': *congressional elections are a biennial phenomenon*. A *biennial plant* is one that lives a two-year cycle, flowering and producing seed in the second year. **Biannual** means 'twice a year': *the solstice is a biannual event*. To avoid confusion, rephrasing is often the best option.

biceps

The form **biceps** works as both a singular and plural noun: *the biceps on his left arm; a pair of bulging biceps.* The singular 'bicep' is a back-formation and is generally viewed as incorrect, as is the plural 'bicepses'. See also NOUNS, SINGULAR AND PLURAL.

billion

The older meaning of **billion** in British English was 'a million million'. However, this meaning has now been almost entirely superseded by the meaning 'a thousand million'.

bipolar disorder

This term is increasingly being used as a more neutral way of referring to what was previously known as **manic depression.** For more information see MANIC DEPRESSION.

black

Evidence for the use of **black** to refer to African peoples (and their descendants) dates back at least to the late 14th century. Although the word has been in continuous use ever since, other terms have been favoured in the past. In the US **coloured** was the term adopted in preference by emancipated slaves following the American Civil War. **Coloured** was itself superseded in the US in the early 20th century by **Negro** as the word preferred by prominent black American campaigners such as Booker T. Washington. In Britain, on the other hand, **coloured** was the most widely used and accepted word in the 1950s and early 1960s. With the civil rights and Black Power movements of the 1960s, **black** was adopted by Americans of African origin to signify a sense of racial pride, and it remains the most widely used and generally accepted term in Britain today. It has been written with a capital letter—**Black**—as a way of indicating that it is a racial description rather than just a colour, but that is not now considered necessary. See also AFRICAN AMERICAN.

blatant

Blatant, a word invented by Spenser in the 16th century, generally refers to bad behaviour which is done openly: *a blatant lie* is one which is very obviously a lie.

Flagrant also refers to behaviour which is obviously bad or immoral, and is often applied to concrete breaches of laws, rules, and regulations: *a flagrant violation of school rules*. Nowadays there is considerable overlap in meaning between them, with **blatant** often applied to such breaches, though purists will maintain the distinction. The adverb **blatantly** (unlike **flagrantly**) has developed a weakened meaning, especially in youth slang, as a stock form of intensifier like **absolutely** and **extremely**: *this song is blatantly subtle*.

blind

It is better to avoid using *the blind* to refer to people in society with sight problems. Instead you should refer to *visually impaired people* or *blind or partially sighted people*.

blond, blonde

The alternative spellings **blond** and **blonde** correspond to the masculine and feminine forms in French, but in English the same distinction is not applied, and either form is therefore correct. Thus, **blond woman**, **blonde woman**, **blond man**, and **blonde man** are all used, though overall **blonde** is the commoner of the two spellings. American usage since the 1970s has generally preferred **blond**, thereby making it gender-neutral.

bona fide, bona fides

Bona fide is an adjectival phrase meaning 'in good faith' and hence 'genuine': *a bona fide tourist*. **Bona fides** is a noun phrase meaning 'good faith' and hence 'sincerity and honesty of intention': *he was at pains to establish his liberal bona fides*. Be careful not to spell them 'bone fide' or 'bone fides'. The pronunciation is /**boh**-nuh **fI**-dee(z)/.

bored

The normal construction for **bored** is **bored by** or **bored with**. More recently, **bored of** has emerged (probably by analogy with other construction, such as **tired of**), but **bored of**, though common in informal English, is not yet considered acceptable in standard English.

born, borne

On the difference between **born** and **borne**, see BEAR.

both

When **both** is used in constructions with **and**, the structures following each should be symmetrical in well-formed English. Accordingly, *studies of lions, both in the wild and in captivity* is better than, for example, *studies of lions, both in the wild and captivity*. In the second example, the symmetry of 'in the wild' and 'in captivity' has been lost.

brackets

The word **brackets** is often applied generally to types which have more specific names: () are **round brackets** or **parentheses**; [] are **square brackets**; {} are **curly brackets** or **braces**; <> are **angle brackets**. When editing or describing documents it may be confusing if you use the general word when you mean a specific type of bracket. In particular, it is useful to remember that in US English **brackets** often means 'square brackets'.

Britain, Great Britain, the British Isles, England

The way these terms are used can be confusing. Some of them have an exact political or legal status, while others are used more loosely.

1 **The British Isles** is the traditional geographical term for the group of islands consisting of Great Britain and Ireland and the smaller islands around them, such as the Hebrides, Orkney, Shetland, the Scilly Isles, the Channel Islands, and the Isle of Man. Nowadays, many people, especially the Irish, prefer the term **Britain and Ireland**.

2 **Great Britain** refers to the largest island in the British Isles, divided between England, Scotland, and Wales. Politically, it means these three countries (since ▶

the Act of Union of 1707), but excludes Northern Ireland, the Isle of Man, and the Channel Islands.

3 **The United Kingdom** is a political term, short for **the United Kingdom of Great Britain and Northern Ireland**. It includes those two countries but not usually the Isle of Man or the Channel Islands.

4 **Britain** is a term with no official status. Sometimes it is used to mean the same as **Great Britain**. Government and media often use it to mean the **United Kingdom** (i.e. including Northern Ireland). While the word **British** has no defined legal status, it is often used as a shorthand for matters relating to the whole United Kingdom, as in *British government, British troops, the British public,* and so forth.

5 **England** strictly refers to a single political division of Great Britain, excluding Wales and Scotland. Less enlightened English people frequently and lamentably say or write **England** when they mean **(Great) Britain**, and using the word in this way can be rather offensive to the Welsh and Scots. This incorrect shorthand is very often used by English-speakers outside the British Isles, and by speakers of other languages. The same is true of the word **English**.

6 To refer in general to a citizen of the United Kingdom, **Briton** is the normal word in British English, and **Britisher** in American English.

broadcast

The verb **broadcast**, by analogy with **cast**, does not change in its past form and past participle: *the programme will be broadcast on Saturdays*. The form 'broadcasted' is not generally considered correct.

bruschetta

If you want to refer to this topped slice of Italian rustic bread approximately as an Italian would, pronounce it /broo-**sket**-uh/, with a short pause before the **t** sound, and spell it with *-sch-* not

-*sh*- in the middle. However, so many people pronounce it as /broo-**shet**-uh/ that this seems likely to be the pronunciation that will establish itself.

bullet points

People are often not sure how to write and punctuate text which uses bullet points. As bullet points are relatively recent, it is hardly surprising that there are no hard-and-fast rules. Also, much depends on each person's visual sensibility, the medium in which bullet points are being used, and the intended audience. The following advice is offered merely as a rule of thumb. If the text of the bullet point is not itself a full sentence, it need not begin with a capital letter and should not finish with a full stop, e.g.

- annual review of capital gains issues

If you prefer to punctuate your list, you should finish each point that is not a complete sentence with a semi-colon, and put a full stop after the last one, e.g.

- annual review of capital gains issues;
- outstanding inheritance tax issues;
- changes in tax regulations.

If the bullet point is a complete sentence, a full stop at the end is technically correct, but might look a bit fussy, e.g.

- This will involve a review of the whole procedure.

You should bear in mind that in an electronic presentation, where you may have few complete sentences, punctuation at the end of bullet points may clutter the look. In other written material you should consider the overall look of the document, the number of bullet points, and their length. You will also need to gauge your audience: lecturers in an English department might be fussier about punctuation than other audiences.

burned, burnt

Both **burned** and **burnt** are used for the past tense and past participle of **burn** and are equally correct. **Burned** is much more common for the past tense, e.g.: *she burned her hand on the kettle*; *the church burned down in 1198*. As a past participle, **burned** and **burnt** are equally common in British English, e.g.: *she had burned herself on the wax*; *the place was burnt to a crisp*, but **burned** is found elsewhere. When the participle is used as an adjective, however, **burnt** is somewhat commoner in all varieties of English: *walls of burnt brick*.

but

For advice about using **but** and other conjunctions to begin a sentence, see AND.

caesarean

The spelling **caesarean**, ending with **-ean** (or **cesarean** in the US), is now much more commonly used than **caesarian** with an **i** and is the generally accepted form.

cafe

There are two ways of pronouncing **cafe**. Americans generally stress the second syllable (/ka-**fay**/) and British English speakers the first (/**ka**-fay/). British English speakers who stress the second syllable run the risk of sounding bizarre or affected. Omitting the accent over the letter **e** is nowadays perfectly legitimate, and is the spelling recommended by Oxford dictionaries. Nevertheless, not all dictionaries recognize that spelling and some people may consider it a mistake to leave out the accent.

can

People are often unclear whether there is any difference between **may** and **can** when used to request or express permission, as in *may/can I ask you a few questions?* It is still widely held that using **can** for permission is somehow incorrect, and that it should be reserved for expressions to do with capability, as in *can you swim?* Although using **can** to request or give permission is not regarded as incorrect in standard English, there is a clear difference in formality between the two verbs: **may** is a more polite way of asking for something and is the better choice in more formal contexts.

candelabrum

If we stick religiously to the Latin forms, the correct singular is **candelabrum** and the correct plural is **candelabra**. But **candelabra** has taken on a new life as the more common singular form, with its own plural **candelabras**.

cannot

Both the one-word form **cannot** and the two-word form **can not** are correct, but **cannot** is far more common in all contexts; in the Oxford English Corpus, there are 25 times more examples of **cannot** than of **can not**. The two-word form is recommended only when **not** is part of a set phrase, such as 'not only... but (also)': *Paul can not only sing well, he also paints brilliantly*.

Caribbean

The word **Caribbean** can be pronounced in two different ways. The first, which is more common in British English, puts the emphasis on the -**be**- (/ka-ri-**bee**-uhn/), while the second, heard in the US and the Caribbean itself, emphasizes the -**ri**- (/kuh-**ri**-bee-uhn/).

Caucasian

In the racial classification developed by Blumenbach and others in the 19th century, **Caucasian** (or **Caucasoid**) included peoples whose skin colour ranged from light (in northern Europe) to dark (in parts of North Africa and India). Although the classification is outdated and the categories are now not generally accepted as scientific (see MONGOLOID), the term **Caucasian** has acquired a more restricted meaning. It is now used, especially in the US, as a synonym for 'white or of European origin', as in *the police are looking for a Caucasian male in his forties*.

Celtic

Celt and **Celtic** can be pronounced with the first letter **c** sounding like either **k-** or **s-**, but the normal pronunciation is with a **k-**, except in the name of the Glaswegian football club.

censure, censor

Censure and **censor**, although quite different in meaning, are frequently confused. To **censure** means 'to express severe disapproval of' (*the country was censured for human rights abuses*), while to **censor** means 'to examine (a book, film, etc.) and suppress unacceptable parts of it': *the letters she received were censored*. Avoid writing **censure** when you mean **censor**, as in the incorrect *the film was censured*.

cervical

Cervical means 'relating to the cervix' (the neck of the womb). With the advent of cervical screening and cervical smears the word has become part of general language. Its pronunciation in general use tends to be /**ser**-vi-k'l/and in medical circles /suh-**vI**-k'l/.

chair, chairman, chairwoman, chairperson

The word **chairman**, which combines connotations of power with grammatical gender bias, was a key word in feminist sensitivities about language. **Chairwoman** dates from the 17th century, but it was hardly a recognized name until the 19th century, and even then it did not solve the problem of how to refer neutrally to a **chairman/chairwoman** when the gender was unknown or irrelevant. Two gender-neutral alternatives emerged in the 1970s: **chairperson** and **chair**, although **chair** was already in use to mean 'the authority invested in a chairman'. **Chair** seems to be more popular than **chairperson**, partly because it seems less contrived and less obviously gender-neutral. See also -PERSON.

chaise longue, chaise lounge

Chaise longue comes from French, literally 'a long chair', with *longue* being the feminine form of the French adjective *long*.

Since it has a very un-English spelling and pronunciation, it has been transformed by folk etymology into the logical **chaise lounge** in the US, where it is the accepted and dominant form. See also FOLK ETYMOLOGY.

challenged

The use with a preceding adverb, e.g. **physically challenged**, was originally intended to give a more positive tone than words such as **disabled** or **handicapped**. It arose in the US in the 1980s and quickly spread to the UK and elsewhere. Despite the originally serious intention the word rapidly became stalled by uses whose intention was to make fun of the attempts at euphemism and whose tone was usually clearly ironic: mocking examples include *cerebrally challenged*, *conversationally challenged*, and *follicularly challenged*. See also DISABLED.

chastise

Chastise is correctly spelled *-ise*, never *-ize*.

cherub

Cherub has the Hebrew plural **cherubim**, pronounced /**che**-ruh-bim/, when referring to angelic beings, and **cherubs** when referring to adorable children. Since **cherubim** is already plural, the form 'cherubims' is unnecessary. The adjective **cherubic** is pronounced /chuh-**roo**-bik/.

Chicano

The term **Chicano** (borrowed from Mexican Spanish and derived from the Spanish word *mejicano*, meaning 'Mexican'), and its feminine form **Chicana**, became current in the early 1960s, first used by politically active groups. **Chicano** and **Chicana** are still in frequent use but have become less politicized. However, Mexican-Americans with less militant political views might find the words offensive. **Hispanic** is a more generic word denoting people in the US of Latin-American or Spanish descent. See also HISPANIC.

chimera

The recommended spelling for this word for a mythological being, an illusory hope or a genetic mix is **chimera** not **chimaera**, and the recommended pronunciation is /ky-**meer**-uh/.

chord, cord

1 There are two distinct words spelled **chord**: (1) in music, a group of notes sounded together to form the basis of harmony, and (2) a technical word in mathematics and engineering, meaning 'a straight line joining the ends of an arc, the leading and trailing edges of an aircraft wing, etc.' The idiom **to strike a chord** derives, somewhat surprisingly, from the technical meaning.

2 The word **cord** meaning 'string, rope, etc.' is used in **spinal cord**, **umbilical cord**, **vocal cord**, etc. The anatomical meaning is often spelled **chord**, particularly in the phrase **vocal chords**, but this spelling is not recommended.

chorizo

Chorizo is a word English has borrowed from Spanish to describe a kind of highly spiced pork sausage. British and American dictionaries suggest the pronunciation (/chuh-**ree**-zoh/) as the standard. You can also pronounce the **z** as an **s**: /chuh-**ree**-soh/. Some people, including famous cooks, pronounce the **z** as in *pizza*: /chuh-**ree**-tsoh/. If you wish to impress by mimicking the pronunciation of the language from which a word comes, it is wise to make sure you choose the right language.

Christian name

In recognition of the fact that English-speaking societies have many religions and cultures, not just Christian ones, the term **Christian name** has largely given way, at least in official contexts, to alternative terms such as **given name**, **first name**, or **forename**.

circumcise

Circumcise is correctly spelled *-ise*, never *-ize*.

classic, classical

Traditionally, **classic** means either 'outstanding', as in *a classic novel*, or 'very typical and representative of its kind', as in *a classic little black dress, a classic example*. **Classical** generally means 'relating to Greek or Roman antiquity' or 'relating to serious or conventional music': *the museum was built in the classical style; he plays jazz as well as classical violin.* Often **classical** is mistakenly used when **classic** is more appropriate: *a classical example* would be one taken from Greek or Latin whereas *a classic example* is the most typical example of its kind.

cleft lip

Cleft lip is the standard accepted term and should be used instead of **harelip**, which is likely to cause offence.

cliché

See OVERUSED WORDS.

climactic, climatic

Climactic means 'forming a climax', as in *the film's climactic battle sequence*. **Climatic** means 'relating to climate', as in *a wide range of climatic conditions*. **Climactic** is sometimes incorrectly used when **climatic** is meant, as *in harsh climactic conditions*. **Climacteric** is a different word again, a rarely used noun meaning 'the period of life when fertility and sexual activity are in decline' or a 'critical period or event'.

clique

Clique, 'a small group of people who spend time together and do not let others join them', is among the thousands of English words purloined from French. If English speakers use French words a lot, they usually alter the pronunciation: it would be very affected indeed to pronounce **clairvoyant** as the French do. But it is better to say **clique** with the French-like pronunciation /kleek/, rather than /klik/, to avoid confusion with **click**.

co-

1 In modern American English, the tendency increasingly is to write compound words beginning with **co-** without hyphenation, as in *costar*, *cosignatory*, and *coproduce*. British usage generally shows a preference for the hyphenated spelling, but even in Britain the trend seems to be in favour of less hyphenation than in the past. In both the US and the UK, for example, the spellings of *coordinate* and *coed* are encountered with or without hyphenation, but the more common choice for either word in either country is without the hyphen.

2 **Co-** with the hyphen is often used to prevent a mistaken first impression (*co-driver*—because *codriver* could be mistaken for *cod river,* and *coworker* initially looks like something to do with a cow), or simply to avoid an awkward spelling (*co-own* is clearly preferable to *coown*). There are also some relatively less common words, such as *co-respondent* (in a divorce suit), where the hyphenated spelling distinguishes the word's meaning and pronunciation from that of the more common *correspondent*.

cohort

The earliest meaning of **cohort** is 'a unit of men within the Roman army'. From this it developed the meanings of 'a group of people with a shared characteristic', e.g. *the Church in Ireland still has a vast cohort of weekly churchgoers*. From the 1950s onwards a new meaning developed in the US, meaning 'a companion or colleague', as in *young Jack arrived with three of his cohorts*. Although this meaning is well established (it accounts for most of the uses of this word in the Oxford English Corpus), there are still some people who object to it on the grounds that **cohort** should only be used for groups of people, never for individuals.

coleslaw

The first part of this word is correctly spelled *cole-*, not *cold-*. **Cole-** is from Dutch *kool* 'cabbage'. It has been replaced by *cold* through a process of FOLK ETYMOLOGY.

C

collective noun

A **collective noun** is a singular noun which refers to a group of people, such as **family**, **committee**, **government**, **BBC**, **NATO**. Collective nouns can be used with either a singular or a plural verb: *my **family was** always hard-working*; *his **family were** disappointed in him*. With a singular verb you are emphasizing the group; with a plural verb, the individuals in the group. Generally speaking, in the US it is more usual for collective nouns to be followed by a singular verb. Bear in mind that any following pronouns or adjectives must be singular or plural like the verb: *the government **is** prepared to act, but not until **it** knows the outcome of the latest talks* (not *. . . until they know the outcome . . .*); *the family have all moved back into their former home.*

coloured (US colored)

The use of **coloured** to refer to skin colour is first recorded in the early 17th century and was adopted by emancipated slaves in the US as a term of racial pride after the American Civil War. In Britain it was the accepted term until the 1960s, when it was superseded (as in the US) by **black**. The term **coloured** lost favour among blacks during this period and is now widely regarded as offensive except in historical contexts. In South Africa, the term **coloured** (also written **Coloured**) has a different history. It is used to refer to people of mixed-race parentage rather than, as elsewhere, African peoples and their descendants. In modern use in this context the word is not considered offensive or derogatory.

communal

Americans tend to stress the second syllable (/kuh-**myoo**-n'l/) and British English speakers the first (/**ko**-myoo-n'l/). The American pronunciation is rapidly gaining ground in Britain, but still grates on the ears of many.

compact

Compact as an adjective can be stressed on the first or second syllable: /**kom-**pakt/ or /kuhm-**pakt**/. Both are correct, but there is a preference for the first in the phrase **compact disc**.

C

comparable

Although the traditional pronunciation of **comparable** in standard British English is with the emphasis on the first syllable rather than the second (/**kom**-pruh-b'l/), an alternative pronunciation with the emphasis on the second syllable (/kuhm-**pa**-ruh-b'l/) is gaining in currency. Both pronunciations are used in American English.

comparatively

The use of **comparatively** in contexts such as *there were comparatively few casualties* has been criticized in the past on the grounds that there is no explicit comparison being made. Even so, there is an implicit one, even if very vague: for instance, in the example above, the comparison is presumably with other incidents or battles. **Comparatively** has been used like this since the early 19th century and to use it in this way is acceptable in standard English.

compare

1 People are sometimes unclear about whether there is any difference between **compare with** and **compare to**, and, if so, whether one is more correct than the other. There is a slight difference. It is usual to use **to** rather than **with** when describing the resemblance, by analogy, of two quite different things, as in *Shall I compare thee to a summer's day?* In the other sense, 'to make a detailed comparison of', it is traditionally held that **with** is more correct than **to**, as in *schools compared their facilities with those of others in the area*. However, in practice the distinction is not clear-cut and both **compare with** and **compare to** are used in either context.

2 In intransitive uses, e.g. *but of all these friends and lovers, there is no one compares with you* (The Beatles, *In My Life*) **with** is the usual preposition in British English, whereas in the US it is **to**, as exemplified in *nothing compares to you*.

complacent, complaisant

Complacent and **complaisant** are two words which are similar in pronunciation and which both come from the Latin verb *complacere* 'to please', but which in English do not mean the same thing. **Complacent** is the commoner word and means 'smug and self-satisfied'. **Complaisant**, on the other hand, means 'willing to please', as in *the local people proved complaisant and cordial*.

complement, compliment

Complement and **compliment**, together with **complementary** and **complimentary**, are frequently confused. Pronounced in the same way, they have quite different meanings. As a verb **complement** means 'to add to something in a way that enhances or improves', as in *a relaunched website will complement the radio programmes*. To remember that this meaning has an **e** before the **m** it may help if you think of **complete**, to which it is related. **Compliment** means 'to admire and praise someone for something', as in *he complimented her on her appearance*, and is often wrongly used where **complement** is the correct spelling. **Complimentary** means 'expressing a compliment' as in *he made lots of complimentary remarks about her*. From this meaning comes the sense of 'given free' as in *honeymooners receive complimentary fruit and flowers*.

complete

On the question of whether you should say *very complete*, *more complete*, etc., see UNIQUE.

compliment

Compliment and **complimentary** are quite different in meaning from **complement** and **complementary.** See COMPLEMENT.

compound

The verb **compound** in its meaning 'to make something bad worse', as in *this compounds their problems*, has an interesting history. It arose through a misinterpretation of the legal phrase **compound a felony**, which, strictly speaking, means 'not to prosecute a felony, in exchange for money or some other consideration'. This led to the use of **compound** in legal contexts to mean 'make something bad worse', which then became accepted in general usage as well.

C

comprise

1 **Comprise** mainly means 'consist of', as in *the country comprises twenty states*. It can also mean 'constitute or make up a whole', as in *this single breed comprises 50 per cent of the Swiss cattle population*. Sentences like the first example can be put in the passive—*the country is comprised of twenty states*—and this is standard English. However, the construction **comprise of**, as in *the property comprises of bedroom, bathroom, and kitchen*, is regarded as incorrect.

2 For a comparison of **comprise** and **include**, see INCLUDE.

concerned

The idiomatic expression **as far as ... is/are concerned** is well established and is a useful way of introducing a new topic or theme or of stating your opinion, especially in conversation. But it can also sometimes be unnecessary or long-winded: for example, *the punishment does not seem to have any effect so far as the prisoners are concerned* could be more economically expressed as *the punishment does not seem to have any effect on the prisoners*.

conjoined twins

The more accurate and correct term **conjoined twins** has supplanted the older term **Siamese twins** in all contexts other than informal conversation.

connote

Connote does not mean the same as **denote**. **Denote** refers to the literal, primary meaning of something, while **connote** refers to other characteristics suggested or implied by that thing. So, you might say that a word like *mother* **denotes** a woman who is a parent but **connotes** qualities such as protection and affection.

consummate

Consummate is pronounced /**kon**-syoo-mayt/ as a verb, e.g. *the marriage was never consummated*. As an adjective meaning 'complete, perfect', e.g. *a consummate liar; consummate* *elegance* it was traditionally pronounced /kuhn-**sum**-uht/, with the emphasis on the second syllable, but the pronunciation /**kon**-syuu-muht/, with the emphasis on the first syllable, is now standard.

contagious

In practice, there is little or no difference in meaning between **contagious** and **infectious** when applied to disease: both mean, roughly, 'communicable'. There is, however, a difference in emphasis or focus between the two words. **Contagious** tends to be focused on the person or animal affected by the disease (*precautions are taken with anyone who seems contagious*), while **infectious** emphasizes the agent or organism which carries the disease: there are, for example, plenty of examples in the Oxford English Corpus of *infectious agent* but none of *contagious agent*.

continual, continuous

There is some overlap in meaning between **continuous** and **continual**, but there is also a useful distinction between them. Both can mean roughly 'without interruption' (*a long and continual war*; *five years of continuous warfare*), but **continuous** is much more prominent in this sense. Also, unlike **continual**, it can be used to refer to space as well as time, as in *the development forms a continuous line along the coast*. **Continual**, on the other hand, typically means 'happening frequently, but with intervals between', as in *continual breakdowns, continual arguments*. Overall, **continuous** occurs much more frequently than **continual** (around six times more often in the Oxford English Corpus) and is found in many technical and specialist uses ranging from grammar and education to mathematics.

contribute

In British English there are two possible pronunciations of the word **contribute**, one which emphasizes the first syllable (/**kon**-trib-yoot/) and one which emphasizes the second (/kuhn-**trib**-yoot/); /kuhn-**trib**-yoot/ is held to be the standard, correct pronunciation, even though /**kon**-trib-yoot/ is older.

controversy

There are two possible pronunciations of the word **controversy** in British English: /**kon**-truh-ver-si/ and /kuhn-**trov**-uh-si/. The latter, though common, is still widely held to be incorrect in standard English.

convince

Using **convince** with an infinitive as a synonym for **persuade** first became common in the 1950s in the US, as in *she **convinced** my father **to** branch out on his own*. Some traditionalists deplore the blurring of the distinction between **convince** and **persuade**. They maintain that **convince** should be reserved for situations in which someone's belief is changed but no action is taken as a result (*he **convinced** me **that** he was right*), while **persuade** should be used for situations in which action results (*he **persuaded** me* rather than *he convinced me **to** seek more advice*). In practice, **convince someone to do something** is well established, and few people will be vexed by its use.

cord

On the confusion between **cord** and **chord**, see CHORD.

could

For a discussion of the use of **could of** instead of **could have**, See HAVE.

councillor, counsellor (US councilor, counselor)

Confusion often arises between the words **counsellor** and **councillor**. A **counsellor** is a person who gives advice or *counsel*, especially on personal problems (*a marriage counsellor*), whereas a **councillor** is a member of a city, county, or other *council* (*she stood as a Labour candidate for city councillor*).

covert

In British English, **covert**, meaning 'secret, disguised', is traditionally pronounced like *cover* (/**kuv**-ert/), although the US pronunciation like *over* (/**koh**-vert/) is gaining ground in Britain and elsewhere.

credible, creditable

Confusion often arises between the words **credible** and **creditable**. **Credible** chiefly means 'convincing' (*few people found his story credible*), while **creditable** means 'praiseworthy' (*their 32nd placing was still a creditable performance, considering they had one of the smallest boats*).

creep

The past tense and past participle of **creep** can be either **crept** or **creeped**, but **crept** is much more often used for both. **Creeped** occurs most commonly in US English.

crescendo

Crescendo in Italian means literally 'growing', and was originally a musical term for a gradual increase in loudness, building to a climax. It has since developed further to mean the resulting state and is widely used to mean 'peak' or 'climax': *demands for a public inquiry rose to a crescendo last week*. Some traditionalists are against this extension of its meaning, but it is now well established.

cripple

The word **cripple** has long been in use and is recorded in the *Lindisfarne Gospels* as early as AD 950. It has now acquired offensive connotations and has been largely replaced by broader terms such as 'person with disabilities'. Similar changes have affected **crippled**; see DISABLED.

criterion

The traditional singular form (following the original Greek) is **criterion**, and the plural form is **criteria**. It is a common mistake, however, to use **criteria** as if it were a singular, as in *a further criteria needs to be considered*, and this use is best avoided. For other examples of this kind of mistake, see NOUNS, SINGULAR AND PLURAL.

critique

Critique is pronounced with emphasis on the second syllable, /kri-**teek**/, and means 'a detailed critical essay or analysis' especially of a literary, political, or philosophical theory: *Kant's Critique of Pure Reason*. Although it may not be liked by some, **critique** is now also regularly used as a verb, especially in the arts world, in a general sense of 'to review' or even just 'to criticize', as in *my writing has been critiqued as being too academic*. For further examples, see VERBS FORMED FROM NOUNS.

c
d

dangling participle

A **participle** is a form of a verb ending in **-ing**, **-ed**, etc., such as *arriving* or *arrived*. A **dangling participle** is one which is left 'hanging' because, in the grammar of the clause, it does not relate to the noun it should relate to. In the sentence ***Arriving** at the station, **she** picked up her case*, the construction is correct because the participle *arriving* and the subject *she* relate to each other (*she* is the one doing the *arriving*). But in the following sentence, a **dangling participle** has been created: ***Arriving** at the station, **the sun** came out*. We know, logically, that it is not the sun which is arriving, but grammatically that is exactly the link which has been created. Such errors are frequent, even in written English, and can give rise to genuine confusion.

data

In Latin, **data** is the plural of **datum** and, historically and in specialized scientific fields, it is also treated as a plural in English, taking a plural verb, as in *the **data were** collected and classified*. In modern non-scientific use, however, it is treated as a mass noun, similar to a word like *information*, which cannot normally have a plural and which takes a singular verb. Sentences such as ***data was** collected over a number of years* are now the norm in standard English and are perfectly correct.

deaf mute

In modern use **deaf mute** has acquired offensive connotations (implying, wrongly, that such people are without the capacity for communication). It should be avoided in favour of other terms such as 'deaf without speech'.

decade

d

1 There are two possible pronunciations for **decade**: one puts the emphasis on the first syllable (/**de**-kayd/) while the other puts it on the second syllable (/di-**kayd**/, like *decayed*). The second pronunciation is disapproved of by some traditionalists but is now regarded as a standard, acceptable alternative.

2 It is good style not to write individual decades with an apostrophe: *during the eighties* or *the 80s*, not *the 'eighties* or *the '80s*.

deceptively

Deceptively belongs to a small set of words whose meaning is rather ambiguous. It can be used in similar grammatical contexts to suggest either one thing or its complete opposite. This happens because people use **deceptively** in two rather different ways. For example, is *a **deceptively** smooth surface* smooth or not? The answer is that it *appears* to be smooth, but in reality is not. So, in this case **deceptively** means something like 'apparently' or 'misleadingly'. But this is the reverse of its use, beloved by estate agents, in phrases such as *a **deceptively** spacious room*. If we follow the logic of the first example, this would mean that the room *looks* spacious, but in fact isn't. And that is the exact opposite of the meaning intended. We can all easily understand what is meant in this sort of example without going to the trouble of analysing it. But often what is being stated really is rather unclear. If you describe a person as *deceptively complex*, is he complex while seeming straightforward, or straightforward while seeming to be complex? To avoid confusion, it is probably best not to use **deceptively** at all when it may be ambiguous, as in the last example.

defining relative clauses

See RELATIVE CLAUSES.

d

definite, definitive

Definitive is often used, rather imprecisely, when **definite** is actually intended, to mean simply 'clearly decided'. Although **definitive** and **definite** have a clear overlap in meaning, **definitive** has the additional meaning of 'having an authoritative basis'. A *definitive decision* is one that is not only conclusive but also carries the stamp of authority or is a benchmark for the future, but a *definite decision* is simply one that has been made clearly and is without doubt.

defuse

On the potential confusion between **defuse** and **diffuse**, see DIFFUSE.

deliver

Deliver is often used to mean 'provide something that you have promised or that people expect of you' as in *the failure of successive governments to deliver economic growth* or *if you can't deliver improved sales figures, you're fired*. While this meaning is well established and was once a lively metaphor, it now runs the risk of being hackneyed and vague. Words you could use instead include **provide** and **supply**. Or you could rewrite your sentence to be more precise and specific about what you mean.

denote

For an explanation of the difference between **denote** and **connote**, see CONNOTE.

depends

In informal use, it is quite common for the *on* to be dropped in sentences such as *it all depends how you look at it* (rather than *it all depends on how you look at it*), but in well-formed written English the *on* should always be retained.

dependant, dependent

Until recently, the only correct spelling of the noun in British English was **dependant**, as in *a single man with no dependants*. However, in modern British English (and in US English), **dependent** is now a standard alternative. The adjective is always spelled **-ent**, never **-ant**, as in *we are dependent on his goodwill*.

deprecate, depreciate

The similarity in spelling and meaning of **deprecate** and **depreciate** has led to confusions in their use, with **deprecate** being used simply as a synonym for **depreciate** in the meaning 'disparage or belittle'. This use is now well established and is widely accepted in standard English. In particular, the phrases **self-deprecating** and **self-deprecatory** are far more common than the alternatives **self-depreciating** and **self-depreciatory**.

derisory

Although the words **derisory** and **derisive** share similar roots, they have different core meanings. **Derisory** usually means 'ridiculously small or inadequate', as in *a derisory pay offer* or *the security arrangements were derisory*. **Derisive**, on the other hand, is used to mean 'expressing contempt'. The proper reaction to a *derisory salary increase* is a *derisive laugh*.

descendant, descendent

In British English, the only way to spell the noun meaning 'a person descended from a particular ancestor' is with the ending **-ant**, as in *property is inherited by descendants of the original owner*. In US English you can spell it that way, or with a final **-ent**.

dice, die

Historically, **dice** is the plural of **die**, but in modern standard English **dice** is both the singular and the plural: *throw the dice* could refer to either one or more than one dice.

different

Different from, **different than**, and **different to**: many people wonder if there is any distinction between these three phrases, and whether one is more correct than the others. In practice, **different from** is by far the most common structure, both in the UK and North America, while **different than** is almost exclusively used in North America. **Different to** is also correct, but is not used as often as either **different from** or **different than**. Since the 18th century, **different than** has been singled out by critics as incorrect, but it is difficult to sustain the view in modern standard English that one version is more correct than the others. There is little difference in meaning between the three, and all of them are used by respected writers.

differently abled

Differently abled was first proposed in the 1980s as an alternative to **disabled**, **handicapped**, etc. on the grounds that it gave a more positive message and so avoided discrimination towards people with disabilities. The term has gained little currency, however, and has been criticized as both over-euphemistic and condescending. The accepted word in general use is still **disabled**. See also DISABILITY, THE LANGUAGE OF.

diffuse, defuse

The verbs **diffuse** and **defuse** sound similar but have different meanings. **Diffuse** means, broadly, 'to disperse', while **defuse** means 'to reduce the danger or tension in'. Sentences such as *they successfully diffused the situation* are wrong, while *they successfully defused the situation* is correct. The literal meaning of **defuse**, that is 'taking out (**de**-) the fuse' may help you remember the distinction.

dilemma

At its core, a **dilemma** is a situation in which a difficult choice has to be made between equally undesirable alternatives. Informally, it can be used of any difficult situation or problem (as in *the insoluble dilemma of adolescence*), and some people regard this weakened meaning as unacceptable. However, the usage is recorded as early as the first part of the 17th century and is now widespread and becoming far more acceptable, although it is best avoided in formal contexts.

diphtheria, diphthong

In the past, **diphtheria** was pronounced with an f sound representing the two letters ph (as in *telephone*, *physics*, and other '*ph-*' words derived from Greek). Today the most common pronunciation is with a p sound, and it is no longer considered incorrect in standard English . A very similar shift has taken place with the word **diphthong**, which is now also widely pronounced /**dip-**/ rather than /**dif-**/.

disability, the language of

The language that is now generally considered suitable to describe and refer to people with different kinds of physical or mental disabilities is very different from what it was a couple of decades ago. The changes are due partly to the activity of the organizations which promote the interests of particular groups with disabilities, and partly to increased public sensitivity to language that might perpetuate stereotypes and prejudices. Just as most people studiously avoid previously established sexist or racist uses of language, so they are more sensitive to the appropriate way in which to talk about people with disabilities.

If you want to use appropriate language you not only need to avoid words which have been or are being superseded, such as *mongolism* or *backward*, and which are listed below with their more neutral equivalents. You should also try to:

- avoid using *the* + an adjective to refer to the whole group, as in *the blind*, *the deaf*, and so forth. The reasoning behind this is twofold: because the humanity of people with a disability should not be circumscribed by the disability itself ('the disability is not the person'); and that talking about people with a given disability as a group diminishes their individuality. The preferred formulation these days is 'a person with . . .' or 'people with . . .' as in *people with sight problems*, *people with asthma*, or *people with disabilities*.
- avoid using words such as *victim*, *suffer from*, and *wheelchair-bound* which suggest that the person concerned is the helpless object of the disability. ▶

Suitable alternatives to *suffer from* are *have*, *experience*, and *be diagnosed with*. Instead of talking about *victims* you can talk about people who have a particular disability; and instead of *wheelchair-bound* you can say *who use(s) a wheelchair*.

- avoid using words which once related to disabilities and which have now become colloquial, especially as insults, such as *mongoloid*, *mong*, *spastic*, *psycho*, *schizo*, and so forth.

Some of the terms below are better established than others, and some groups with disabilities favour specific words over others. These lists are offered only as a general guide.

OLDER TERM	NEUTRAL TERM
able-bodied	non-disabled
asthmatic (noun)	person with asthma
backward	having learning difficulties, having a learning disability
blind	partially sighted, visually impaired
cripple	person with a disability, person with mobility problems
deaf aid	hearing aid
deaf-and-dumb	deaf without speech
deaf-mute	deaf without speech
diabetic (noun)	person with diabetes
disabled	having a disability
handicapped	having a disability
harelip	cleft lip
to help	to support
invalid	person with a disability
mongol	person with Down's syndrome
spastic	person with cerebral palsy
stone-deaf	profoundly deaf

d

disabled

The word **disabled** came to be used as the standard term in referring to people with physical or mental disabilities from the 1960s onwards, and it remains the most generally accepted term in both British and US English today. It superseded words that are now more or less offensive, such as *crippled*, *defective*, and *handicapped*, and has not been overtaken itself by newer coinages such as *differently abled* or *physically challenged*. Although the usage is very widespread, some people regard making the adjective a plural noun (as in *the needs of the disabled*) as dehumanizing because it tends to treat people with disabilities as an undifferentiated group, defined merely by their capabilities. To avoid offence, a more acceptable term would be 'people with disabilities'.

disassociate

Disassociate is slightly older than its variant **dissociate**, which is first recorded in 1623. **Disassociate** is, however, regarded by some people as an ignorant mistake, being formed regularly like **disassemble**, and it is therefore occasionally best avoided.

disc, disk

Generally speaking, the preferred British spelling is **disc** and the preferred US spelling is **disk**, although there is much overlap and variation between the two. In particular, the spelling for meanings relating to computers is nearly always **disk**, as in *hard disk, disk drive*, and so on. In *compact disc*, however, the spelling with a *c* is more usual.

discomfit, discomfort

The words **discomfit** and **discomfort** are historically unrelated but in modern use their principal meanings as verbs have collapsed into one ('to make someone feel uneasy').

discreet, discrete

The words **discrete** and **discreet** are pronounced in the same way and share the same origin but they do not mean the same thing. **Discrete** means 'separate', as in *a finite number* *of discrete categories*, while **discreet** means 'careful and circumspect', as in *you can rely on him to be discreet*.

disinterested

Nowhere are the battle lines more deeply drawn in usage questions than over the difference between **disinterested** and **uninterested**. According to traditional guidelines, **disinterested** should never be used to mean 'not interested' but only to mean 'impartial', as in *the judgements of disinterested outsiders are likely to be more useful*. Following this view, only **uninterested** means 'not interested', but the 'incorrect' use of **disinterested** is widespread. Nevertheless, in careful writing it is advisable to avoid using it to mean 'not interested' as many people will judge it to be incorrect.

dissociate

For a comparison of **dissociate** and **dissasociate**, see DISASSOCIATE.

distribute

The word **distribute** is pronounced either as /dis-**trib**-yoot/, with the emphasis on the second syllable, or as /**dis**-trib-yoot/, with the emphasis on the first. Until recently, /**dis**-trib-yoot/ was considered incorrect in standard British English, but now both pronunciations are standard.

dive, dove

In British English the standard past tense is **dived**, as in *he ran past us and dived into the water*. In the 19th century **dove** (rhyming with *stove*) occurred in British and American dialect and it remains in regular use. It is more frequent than **dived** in the US and Canada. In Britain it should still be avoided in careful writing.

double negative

According to standard English grammar, it is incorrect to use a **double negative,** i.e. two negative words to express a single negative idea, as in *I don't know nothing*. The rules dictate that the two negative elements cancel each other out to give an affirmative statement, so that *I don't know nothing* would be interpreted as 'I know something'.

In practice this sort of double negative is widespread in dialect and other non-standard usage and rarely gives rise to confusion as to the intended meaning. Double negatives are standard in other languages as diverse as French, Russian, and Afrikaans, and they have not always been unacceptable in English, either. They were normal in Old English and Middle English and did not come to be frowned upon until some time after the 16th century, when attempts were made to relate the rules of language to the rules of formal logic.

Modern (correct) uses of the double negative give an added subtlety to statements: saying *I am* ***not un****convinced by his argument* suggests reservations in the speaker's mind that are not present in its supposedly logical equivalent, *I am convinced by his argument*.

dove

For the use of **dove** as the past tense of **dive**, see DIVE.

Down's syndrome

Of relatively recent coinage, **Down's syndrome** (or, increasingly frequently, **Down syndrome**) is the accepted term in modern use, and former terms, such as **mongol** and **mongolism**, should be avoided as they are highly likely to cause offence. A person with the syndrome is best called exactly that, a **person with Down's syndrome**.

downward, downwards

The only correct form for the adjective is **downward** (*a downward spiral, a downward trend*), but **downward** and **downwards** are both used for the adverb, e.g. *the floor sloped downward/downwards*, with a marked preference for **downwards** in British English and **downward** in American English.

dream

For the past tense and past participle of **dream**, **dreamt** and **dreamed** are both used and are both correct. **Dreamed** is pronounced /dreemd/ (and occasionally /dremt/) and **dreamt** is pronounced /dremt/. For the past tense in British English **dreamt** and **dreamed** are equally common, but in US English **dreamed** is more often used. For the past participle, **dreamed** is used more often in Britain and the US.

due

Using **due to** to mean 'because of', as in *he had to retire due to an injury*, has been condemned as wrong on the grounds that **due** is an adjective, and should therefore refer to a noun or pronoun, e.g. *an illness due to old age*. According to this view, it should not refer to a verb, such as *retire* in the first example above; **owing to** is often recommended as a better alternative. However, the use with a verb, first recorded at the end of the 19th century, is now common in all types of literature and is regarded as part of standard English.

dumb

Although 'not able to speak' is the older meaning of **dumb**, it has been so overwhelmed by the newer meaning of 'stupid' that using it in the first meaning is now almost certain to cause offence. Alternatives such as 'having a speech disorder' are more appropriate.

dwarf

In the meaning 'an abnormally small person', **dwarf** is normally considered offensive. However, there are no accepted alternatives in the general language, since terms such as **person of restricted growth** have gained little currency.

each

People are sometimes confused about whether verbs and possessives following **each** should be singular or plural. **Each** is treated as singular when it comes before a singular noun (***each*** *house* ***stands*** *on its own*), when it is followed by

of and a plural noun (***each** of the houses **stands** on its own*), and when it stands by itself as a pronoun: *a series of interconnecting courtyards, each with its own character.* When **each** follows and qualifies a plural noun or pronoun, e.g. ***they** each **carry** several newspapers; the voices **each have** slight differences in note-lengths*, it is treated as a plural. This is because it is the noun or pronoun and not **each** that determines if the sentence is singular or plural.

ebullient

Ebullient is pronounced /i-**bul**-yuhnt/, with the second syllable as in *bulb*, not as in *bull*.

economic, economical

People sometimes describe something as **economic** when they mean **economical**. **Economic** means 'concerning economics': *he's rebuilding a solid economic base for the country's future.* **Economical** means 'thrifty, avoiding waste': *small cars should be inexpensive to buy and economical to run.*

effect

For an explanation of the difference between **effect** and **affect**, see AFFECT.

egregious

Egregious is an unusual word because its original meaning of 'remarkably good, distinguished' has been ousted by the exact opposite, 'outstandingly bad, shocking'. The word comes from Latin *grex* meaning 'flock', and originally meant 'towering above the flock', i.e. 'prominent'. Now it means 'prominent because bad': *egregious abuses of copyright.*

either

1 In good English writing style, it is important that **either** and **or** are correctly placed so that the structures following each word balance and mirror each other. Accordingly, sentences such as ***either** I accompany you **or** I wait here* and *I'm going to buy **either** a new camera **or** a new video* are correct, whereas sentences such as *either I accompany you or John* and *I'm either going to buy a new camera or a video* are not well-balanced sentences and should not be used in written English.

2 **Either** can be pronounced /**I**-*th*uh/ or /**ee**-*th*uh/: both are correct.

Electronic English

Over the last decade or more our lives have been transformed by electronic communication; arguably our language has been transformed as well. Electronic communication includes several different forms: email, chatrooms, newsgroups, weblogs, and SMS (Short Messaging Service) messages between mobile phones, or 'texts'. In fact, it is probably more accurate to talk about 'Electronic Englishes', since different groups in cyberspace have different jargons and conventions. English in general constantly evolves, and the influence of, for instance, TV and films on the language can be very rapid: take '*am I bothered?*', which became a catchphrase in Britain in 2005. The difference with electronic communication is that a word can be invented and then spread immediately round the world.

Electronic communication is an extremely fertile source of new words, which enter the mainstream if what they refer to takes root. For example, a *blog* (short for *weblog*, a personal website on which someone records or writes about topics of interest to them), of which there are now estimated to be at least twenty million worldwide, is now a well-established word, though only a few years ago it was a completely unknown concept to most people. Similarly, *podcasts* (digital recordings of a radio broadcast or similar programme, made available on the Internet for downloading to a personal audio player) were little known in 2004 but are now part of mainstream media. In the same way, *to google* is in the process of ▶

becoming a generic term for 'to look for information on the web'.

Older forms of communication are renamed to distinguish them from the electronic version, so that *snailmail* refers to traditional postal mail, and *dead tree edition* refers to articles, books, and so forth published on paper rather than in electronic format.

Not only are new words created at a vast rate, new 'dialects' come into being. There has been talk of *globish* and *globespeak*, which are pared down versions of traditional English, with severely limited vocabularies, designed to make it easier for people with different mother tongues to communicate. Similarly, *Leetspeak* is a language which emerged from online gaming communities and users of bulletin boards. It works with a cipher system, such as replacing letters with numbers, transposing letters, and modifying existing words in other ways, so that, for instance 'hacker' can be written as 'haxxor' or 'haxor'.

Apart from producing hundreds of new words every year, 'Electronic English' has also affected the conventions governing the way we write. If we send an email for business purposes, we are likely to be more informal in the way we write it and address the recipient than we would be in a letter or memo. Certain abbreviations which are widely used in text messaging, chatrooms, and so forth are now being widely used in advertising and marketing: *event starts @ 8 o'clock 2moro*, *gr8* (= great), *l8r* (= later), *specially 4 U*, and so forth. Even electronic message signs on motorways will flash up *R U 2 close?* Another effect is that capital letters are less favoured in titles, brand names, and so forth, lower-case letters possibly being seen as less dIstant and authoritarian, and as establishing a more personal connection with the consumer or customer.

elicit

Elicit is sometimes confused with **illicit** because both words are pronounced the same way (/i-**liss**-it/). **Elicit** is a verb meaning 'to extract (an answer, admission, etc.)' whereas **illicit** is an adjective meaning 'unlawful, forbidden', as in *illicit drinking*.

eminent

Some people write **eminent danger** when what they probably mean is **imminent danger**. They may do this because they pronounce the **e** and the **i** at the beginning of the two words similarly. If it means anything at all, 'eminent danger' would be great danger. **Imminent danger** is a danger that will arise very soon.

emotive

The words **emotive** and **emotional** are similar but are not the same. **Emotive** means 'arousing intense feeling', while **emotional** tends to mean 'characterized by intense feeling'. An *emotive issue* is, therefore, one which is likely to arouse people's passions, while an *emotional response* comes from your feelings, not your thoughts.

empathy

Empathy is often used in contexts where **sympathy** would be more appropriate. **Empathy** means 'the ability to understand and share the feelings of another', as in *both authors have the skill to make you feel empathy with their heroines*. **Sympathy** means 'feelings of pity and sorrow for someone else's misfortune', as in *they had great sympathy for the flood victims*.

endear

To **endear** someone **to** someone else means 'to make someone popular with or liked by someone'. The meaning is easy to grasp, but some people get into a bit of a muddle with the grammar. You can **endear yourself to** other people: *she endeared herself to all who worked with her*. Alternatively, a quality someone has, or an action on their part, can **endear** them **to** other people: *Flora's spirit and character endeared her to everyone who met her*.

But to say *his attitude endeared me to him*, when you mean 'made ME like HIM', is to describe who likes whom back to front; it should be *his attitude endeared him to me*.

end of the day

At the end of the day is one of the less attractive clichés of the 20th century. It is first recorded in 1974 and means no more than 'eventually' or 'when all's said and done'. It is now wildly overused in speech as a 'filler' and tends to creep into almost any conversation. It is not good style to use it in writing.

England

For inappropriate use of **England** to mean **Britain**, see BRITAIN, 5.

enormity

Enormity traditionally means the 'extreme scale or seriousness of something bad or wrong', as in *his time in prison has still not been long enough to allow him to come to grips with the enormity of his crime*, but it is not uncommon for it to be used to mean 'hugeness' or 'immensity', as in *the enormity of French hypermarkets*. Many people regard this use as wrong, arguing that as the word originally meant 'crime, wickedness' it should only be used in a negative way, but the newer use is now broadly accepted in standard English.

enquire

Usage guides have traditionally drawn a distinction between **enquire** and **inquire**, suggesting that, in British English at least, **enquire** is used for general meanings of 'to ask', while **inquire** is reserved for uses meaning 'to make a formal investigation'. In practice, however, there is little difference in the way the two words are used, although **enquire** and **enquiry** are more common in British English while **inquire** and **inquiry** are more common in US English.

ensure

On the difference between **ensure** and **insure**, see INSURE.

e

enterprise

Enterprise in modern use is always spelled *-ise*, not *-ize*.

enthuse

The verb **enthuse** was formed by shortening the noun **enthusiasm**. Like many verbs formed from nouns in this way, especially those from the US, traditionalists regard it as unacceptable. It is difficult to see why: forming verbs from nouns is a perfectly respectable means for creating new words in English: verbs like **classify**, **commentate**, and **edit** were also formed in this way, for example. **Enthuse** itself has now been in English for over 150 years. For further information, see VERBS FORMED FROM NOUNS.

envelop, envelope

Envelop, pronounced /in-**vel**-uhp/, is a verb, meaning 'to wrap up, surround, etc.', while **envelope**, pronounced /**en**-vuh-lohp/ (or, increasingly rarely, /**on**-vuh-lohp/), is a noun, meaning 'a container for a letter, etc.'.

equal

It is widely held that adjectives such as **equal** and **unique** should not be modified and that it is incorrect to say **more equal** or **very unique**, on the grounds that these are adjectives which refer to a logical or mathematical absolute. For more information on this question, see UNIQUE.

equally

The construction **equally as**, as in *follow-up discussion is equally as important*, rather than . . . *is equally important*, is relatively common but is condemned on the grounds that it says the same thing twice. Either word can be used alone and be perfectly correct, e.g. *follow-up discussion is equally important* or *follow-up discussion is as important*.

equidistant

To refer to something being the same distance from two other points or places, **equidistant** is traditionally used with

from, as though it were 'equally distant from': *equidistant from Aberdeen and Inverness*. The use of **between** instead, though quite widespread, would be considered incorrect by many people.

erratum

In Latin, the word **erratum** is singular and its plural form is **errata**. In English, this distinction is maintained. It is therefore incorrect to use **errata** as a singular, as in *it was not intended to print an errata*. Similarly, it is wrong to create the form *erratas* as the plural: *to check out the erratas of the book* should be *to check out the errata of the book*. For other examples of this kind of mistake, see NOUNS, SINGULAR AND PLURAL.

escalate

To **escalate** has gained a novel, transitive meaning, which is 'to refer an issue to a manager or superior': *in the event that you need to escalate an issue, our technical staff are ready to help*. It is part of the jargon of IT and call centres, and best avoided outside those rarefied environments.

Eskimo

In recent years, the word **Eskimo** has come to be regarded as offensive (partly through the associations of the now discredited folk etymology 'one who eats raw flesh'). The peoples inhabiting the regions from the central Canadian Arctic to western Greenland prefer to call themselves **Inuit** (see INUIT). The word **Eskimo**, however, continues to be the only term which can be properly understood as applying to the people as a whole and is still widely used in anthropological and archaeological contexts.

especially

Especially and **specially** overlap in use and meaning. Broadly speaking, both words mean 'particularly', and the preference for one word over the other is linked with particular conventions of use rather than with any deep difference in meaning. For example, there is little to choose between *written especially for Jonathan* and *written specially for Jonathan* and neither is more correct than the other. On the other hand, in sentences such as *he despised them all, especially Sylvester*, **specially** is used instead in informal speech but should not be used in written English, while in *the car was specially made for the occasion* **especially** would be somewhat unusual. Overall, **especially** is by far the commoner of the two, occurring more than thirteen times as frequently as **specially** in the Oxford English Corpus.

espresso

The often-occurring variant spelling **expresso** is incorrect and was probably formed by analogy with **express**.

-ess

The suffix **-ess** has been used since the Middle Ages to form nouns denoting female persons, using a neutral or male form as the base (such as **hostess** from **host** or **actress** from **actor**). In the late 20th century many of these feminine forms came to be seen as old-fashioned, sexist, and patronizing, and the 'male' form is increasingly being used as the 'neutral' form, where the gender of the person concerned is simply unspecified because irrelevant. Some *-ess* forms have all but vanished (e.g. **poetess**, **authoress**, **editress**), but some persist in varying degrees, many falling into these categories:

- they denote someone very different from the male 'equivalent' (e.g. **mayoress**, the wife of a mayor, not a female mayor; **governess**, not a female governor; **countess** if she is the wife of an earl; **manageress**, who might manage a restaurant but not a football team, or **hostess**, who could not be the presenter of a television programme
- they are fixed titles (e.g. **princess**)
- the male equivalent word is rather different in form (e.g. **abbess**, **duchess**, **mistress**)
- in a few cases where there has been a completely different expression for the male equivalent, both have given way to new neutral forms; for instance, **air hostesses** and **stewards** are now generally both called **flight attendants**.

estimate

How you should pronounce **estimate** depends on whether you are using it as a noun or a verb. As a noun, as in *our first estimates were too low*, **estimate** is pronounced /**e**-sti-muht/. As a verb it is pronounced /**e**-sti-mayt/, giving the final vowel its full value. Quite often you hear the verb pronounced /**e**-sti-muht/, like the noun, but this is incorrect.

et cetera (also etcetera)

A common mispronunciation of **et cetera** involves replacing the **t** in **et** with a **k**: /ik-**set**-ruh/ instead of /it-**set**-ruh/. This follows a process known technically as 'assimilation' by which sounds become easier for the speaker to make, but careful speakers will tend to avoid pronouncing the word that way.

ethnic

In recent years, **ethnic** has begun to be used in a euphemistic way to refer to non-white people as a whole, as in *a radio station which broadcasts to the ethnic community in Birmingham*. Although this usage is quite common, especially in journalism, it is considered by many to be inaccurate and mealy-mouthed and is better replaced by words such as 'black', 'Asian', etc.

-ette

The use of **-ette** as a feminine suffix for forming new words is relatively recent: it was first recorded in the word **suffragette** at the beginning of the 20th century and has since been used to form only a handful of well-established words, including **usherette** and **drum majorette**, for example. Nowadays, when the tendency is to use words which are neutral in gender, the suffix **-ette** is not very common and new words formed using it tend to be restricted to the deliberately flippant or humorous, as, for example, **bimbette**, **punkette**, and **ladette**.

euphemism

Euphemism is the use of a milder or vaguer word or phrase in place of one that might seem too harsh or direct in a particular context, and **a euphemism** is such a word or phrase, e.g. *to pass away* for 'to die'.

The few examples of common euphemism below give an idea of the richness of this area in English.

lavatory	bog, comfort station, convenience, little boys' room, little house, loo, restroom (N. Amer.), washroom (N. Amer.), water closet
urinate	have a tinkle, pass water, relieve oneself, spend a penny, take a leak
prostitute	call girl, fallen woman, lady of the night, street-walker, working girl
die	depart this life, give up the ghost, kick the bucket, pass away, pass on
kill	do away with, remove, take out, terminate

The most productive subjects for euphemism in English are bodily functions, sexual activity, death, politics, and violence. In the past, religion and god were rich sources of euphemism and gave English many disguised versions of oaths, such as *crikey* (instead of *Christ*) and *gosh* (instead of *God*). Nowadays business, politics, and warfare create a lot of euphemisms, such as *downsizing, rationalization*, *restructuring*, *slimming down*, etc., instead of the more direct 'redundancy'; *strategic alternatives* for 'potential sale'; *ethnic cleansing* instead of 'mass expulsion or extermination of ethnic minorities'; *collateral damage* for 'accidental destruction of non-military areas'; *friendly fire* for 'killing of soldiers on one's own side'; and *extraordinary rendition* for 'handing over terrorist suspects for interrogation and possible torture'.

One area of euphemism that advertisers are particularly fond of is taking a feature of their product that might seem to be a disadvantage and turning it into something neutral or even ▶

positive. For instance, a product that is basic may be described as *standard* or one that is small as *compact*. A small quantity of a product may be described as a *handy version* or *fun size*, and a long-standing design as *traditional* or *classic*.

Euphemism is not confined to single words. Examples of phrases which are in themselves euphemistic are: *helping the police with their inquiries* (= under interrogation and facing imminent arrest), and *tired and emotional* (= drunk).

e

Eurasian

In the 19th century the word **Eurasian** was normally used to refer to a person of mixed British and Indian parentage. In its modern uses, however, the word is more often used to refer to a person of mixed white-American and South-East-Asian parentage.

everybody

Everybody, along with **everyone**, was traditionally followed by a singular possessive adjective or pronoun: *everybody must sign* ***his*** *own name*. Because the use of **his** in this context is now commonly perceived as sexist, a second option has become popular: *everybody must sign* ***his or her*** *own name*. But **his or her** is often awkward, and many people feel that the plural simply makes more sense: *everybody must sign* ***their*** *own name*. Although this violates strict grammar, pairing a singular subject (*everybody*) with a plural possessive determiner (*their*), it is in fact standard in British English and increasingly so in US English. Indeed, in some sentences, only **they** makes grammatical sense: *everybody agreed to convict the defendant, and they voted unanimously*.

everyday

The adjective **everyday**, 'relating to every day; ordinary', is correctly spelled as one word (*carrying out their everyday activities*), but the adverbial phrase **every day**, meaning 'each day', is always spelled as two words: *it rained every day*.

everyone

The pronoun **everyone**, meaning 'every person', is correctly spelled as one word: *everyone had a great time at the party*. The two-word expression **every one** means 'each individual of a group', as in *every one of the employees got a bonus at the end of the year*. The word **everybody** could be used in the first example but not in the second example. See also EVERYBODY.

everyplace

Everyplace is a modern American English synonym of **everywhere**: *they seem to be everyplace we go*. It is thought to be more 'logical' than *everywhere*, mirroring expressions such as *everybody* and *every time*—on the grounds that we don't say *everywho* or *everywhen*!

extraordinary

In British English, **extraordinary** is traditionally pronounced /ik-**stror**-duhn-ri/ as four syllables, the **-a-** being merged into the following **-or-** to form one syllable. The pronunciation as /eks-truh-**or**-din-ri/ is being increasingly heard, based on US pronunciation.

extrovert

The original spelling **extravert** is now rare in general use but is found in technical use in psychology.

farther, farthest

On the difference in use between **farther** and **further**, see FURTHER.

faze

Faze means 'to disconcert or disturb' and is often used informally with a negative word: *the prospect of going on stage for forty minutes does not seem to have fazed her*. In origin it is a 19th-century American English variant of the ancient verb *feeze* 'to drive off, to frighten away' and has nothing to do with the ordinary verb **phase**. The spelling **phase** is now quite common, but it should be avoided in writing.

feasible

The core meaning of **feasible** is 'possible and practical to do easily or conveniently', as in *the Dutch have demonstrated that it is perfectly feasible to live below sea level*. Some traditionalists object to its use to mean 'likely' or 'probable', as in *the most feasible explanation*, on the grounds that it derives from an Old French word meaning literally 'doable'. If English were restricted to the 'literal' or 'original' meanings of words, our vocabulary would probably be halved at a stroke. This use has been in English for centuries, first recorded in the mid 17th century and supported by 'considerable literary authority', according to the *Oxford English Dictionary*. However, it can be advisable to avoid it in formal contexts.

February

To pronounce **February** 'the way it is written' is not easy. It requires the separate pronunciation of both the **r** following the **Feb**- and the **r** in -**ary**, with an unstressed vowel in between: /**feb**-ruu-uh-ri/. As a result, the **r** following **Feb**- has been replaced by a y sound: /**feb**-yuu-ri/. This is now the norm, especially in spontaneous speech, and is fast becoming the accepted standard. (The process that made this happen is technically called 'dissimilation', which means that when identical sounds are close to each other, one of them is replaced by a different sound.)

-fest

-fest is a now well-established suffix derived from the German word *Fest* meaning 'festival, celebration'. It occurred first in American English in the late 19th century in the word **gabfest** meaning 'a gathering for talking' and spread rapidly to produce other words. It is now very freely used and produces words such as **slugfest**, **lovefest**, and **ladyfest**.

fetus

The spelling **foetus** has no etymological basis but is recorded from the 16th century and until recently was the standard British spelling in both technical and non-technical use. In technical usage **fetus** is now the standard spelling throughout the English-speaking world, but **foetus** is still quite commonly found in British English outside technical contexts.

fewer, less

Strictly speaking, the rule is that **fewer**, the comparative form of **few**, is used with words referring to countable things, including people: *fewer books*; *fewer than ten contestants*. **Less**, on the other hand, is used with things which cannot be counted: *less money*; *less music*. In addition, **less** is normally used with numbers when they are on their own, e.g. *less than 10,000*, and with expressions of measurement or time: *less than two weeks*; *less than four miles away*. To use **less** with countable things, as in *less words* or *less people*, is widely regarded as incorrect in standard English. It is a well-known usage point in English—so much so that an upmarket British store chain was forced by public demand to change the check-out signs in its food supermarkets from 'Less than five items' to 'Fewer than five items'.

fictional, fictitious

The distinction between **fictional** and **fictitious** is quite subtle but worth maintaining. **Fictional** means 'occurring in fiction', i.e. in a piece of literature, whereas **fictitious** means 'invented, not genuine'. So *Oliver Twist* is a **fictional** name when it refers to Dickens' character, and a **fictitious** name when someone uses it as a false or assumed name instead of their own. Similarly, events are **fictional** when described in a work of fiction, and **fictitious** when invented in ordinary life.

first, firstly

Some people maintain that when listing a sequence of points or topics you should introduce the first item with **first**, not **firstly**, although you can follow it with **secondly**, **thirdly**,

fourthly, etc. The reason for this is that **first** early on had a role as an adverb, and the use of **firstly**, though established by the 17th century, has been felt to be an unnecessary affectation, derided by, for instance, De Quincey as 'your ridiculous and most pedantic neologism of firstly.' Today this rule seems little more than a superstition, and various sequences are in use:

- *first, . . . , secondly, . . . , thirdly, . . .*
- *firstly, . . . , secondly, . . . , thirdly, . . .*
- *first, . . . , second, . . . , third, . . .*

The one option that is not acceptable is:

- *firstly, . . . , second, . . . , third, . . .*

first name

For **first name** see CHRISTIAN NAME.

fish

The normal plural of **fish** is **fish**: *a shoal of fish*; *he caught two huge fish*. The older form **fishes** is still used to refer to different *kinds* of fish: *freshwater fishes of the British Isles*.

fit

1 For **fit** as a verb, the past tense and past participle in British English are **fitted** in all meanings: *the dress fitted well; the dress fitted her well; we've fitted a new lock to the front door*. In some parts of the US, **fit** can be used in the first two of these three meanings and is perfectly acceptable in US English: *his head fit snugly into his collar; I tried on several jackets, but none fit me*.

2 The British English use of **fit** to mean 'sexually attractive' is still rather slangy. It is therefore best avoided in any kind of language which is not slang. It is also potentially ambiguous in contexts such as *she is really fit*, which many speakers will understand to mean 'she is in peak physical condition'.

flaccid

The pronunciations /**flak-**sid/ and /**flass-**id/ are both standard. /**Flak-**sid/ is the older and more traditional one and enjoys support on the grounds that it follows the rule for other words containing **-cci-** or **-cce-** (*succinct*, *access*, etc.) except those derived from Italian (*cappuccino* etc.).

flagrant

For a comparison of **flagrant** and **blatant**, see BLATANT.

flammable

The words **flammable** and **inflammable** paradoxically mean the same thing: see INFLAMMABLE.

flaunt

Flaunt and **flout** may sound similar but they have different meanings. **Flaunt** means 'to display ostentatiously', as in *visitors who liked to flaunt their wealth*, while **flout** means 'to openly disregard', as in *new recruits growing their hair and flouting convention*. It is a common error, recorded since around the 1940s, to use **flaunt** when **flout** is intended, as in *the young woman had been flaunting the rules and regulations*. Around 20 per cent of the uses of **flaunt** in the Oxford English Corpus are incorrect in this respect.

fleshy, fleshly

Fleshy relates to flesh in its physical sense and means primarily 'plump, fat' (e.g. *fleshy hands*, *fleshy fruit*) whereas **fleshly** relates to the more metaphorical meanings of flesh, and means 'carnal, sensual, sexual', as in *fleshly desires*, *fleshly thoughts*. To use **fleshly** to mean 'plump' or 'fat' will generally be considered incorrect.

floccinaucinihilipilification

Floccinaucinihilipilification, supposedly meaning 'the action or habit of estimating something as worthless', is one of a number of very long words that occur very rarely in genuine use. See also ANTIDISESTABLISHMENTARIANISM.

flounder

For the difference between **flounder** and **founder**, see FOUNDER.

flout

Flout and **flaunt** do not mean the same: see FLAUNT.

foetus

On the spelling of this word, see FETUS.

folk etymology

f

Folk etymology is the name given to the process by which people modify a strange or unfamiliar word or phrase so that they can relate it to a word or phrase they already know. It has produced the modern forms of many words we now take for granted and is still a dynamic process in the development of English, as can be seen from the modern examples below.

There are three main reasons for the modification of the word to take place.

1 The form is foreign, and so is altered to resemble a more familiar or natural-sounding English word or root.

Examples of this are: *crayfish*, from the Middle English and Old French form *crevice*, where the second syllable has been interpreted as 'fish'; *chaise lounge*, the very common form, especially in the US, of the *chaise longue*; and *cockroach*, which used two English words, cock and roach, to turn the odd-sounding *cacarootch* into something more native.

2 Part of the word or phrase has dropped out of use altogether, or has become rather rare, so its meaning is not understood. It is then replaced by a more familiar word which sounds or looks similar.

This happened, for instance, to *bridegroom*, in which 'groom' has nothing to do with horses. The Old English word was *brideguma*, meaning 'bride-man', and over time the second part was re-interpreted. Current examples of this process are the replacement of *moot point* by *mute point*, and *damp squib* by *damp squid*. A related process, which is not strictly speaking folk etymology, is when the spelling of a word or phrase changes because the words are divided ▶

differently from their original form. Classic examples of this are *an adder* from *a naddre*, and *a newt* from *an ewt*. A modern example of this process in operation is the phrase *to all intensive purposes* for *to all intents and purposes*.

3 One element of the word or phrase is interpreted as a different word which sounds exactly the same. Examples of this are *free reign* for *free rein* and *just desserts* for *just deserts*.

Some modern folk etymologies are now so widespread that they are likely to become the dominant and accepted form. The list below shows some of the most frequent, and how often they occur relative to their traditional forms in the Oxford English Corpus.

TRADITIONAL FORM		FOLK ETYMOLOGY	
sleight of hand	85%	slight of hand	15%
fazed by	71%	phased by	29%
home in on	65%	hone in on	35%
a shoo-in	65%	a shoe-in	35%
bated breath	60%	baited breath	40%
free rein	54%	free reign	46%
chaise longue	54%	chaise lounge	46%
buck naked	53%	butt-naked	47%
vocal cords	51%	vocal chords	49%
just deserts	42%	just desserts	58%
fount of knowledge	41%	font of knowledge	59%
strait-laced	34%	straight-laced	66%

following

Following has long been used as an adjective qualifying a noun, as in *for the following reasons*, or as a noun, as in *the following are my reasons*, where the 'reasons' are what is doing the 'following' and are therefore the logical subject of the verb **follow**. From this has developed a use of **following** as a preposition, as in *used car prices are going up, following the Budget*, where 'follow' has no logical subject. This use has been criticized in cases where it merely means 'after' rather than 'as a result of'. In such cases **after** would do equally well, and **following** may sound somewhat pompous. In the example just given there is a strong element of cause and effect, and so the use of **following** is justified. This is not true of *members are invited to take tea in the Convocation Coffee House following the meeting*.

forename

f

See CHRISTIAN NAME.

former

Traditionally, **former** and **latter** are used in relation to pairs of items: either the first of two items (**former**) or the second of two items (**latter**). The reason for this is that **former** and **latter** were formed as comparatives, adjectives which are correctly used when referring to just two things. In practice, **former** and **latter** are now sometimes used just as synonyms for **first** and **last** and are routinely used to refer to a contrast involving more than two items. Such uses, however, are not good English style.

formidable

There are two possible pronunciations of **formidable**: /**for**-mi-duh-b'l/ with the emphasis on the first syllable and /for-**mid**-uh-b'l/ with the emphasis on the second. /for-**mid**-uh-b'l/ is now common in British English, and the traditional pronunciation /**for**-mi-duh-b'l/ is rarely heard nowadays. Both pronunciations are acceptable in modern standard English.

fortuitous

The traditional, historical meaning of **fortuitous** is 'happening by chance': *a fortuitous meeting* is a chance meeting, which might turn out to be either a good thing or a bad thing. Today, however, **fortuitous** tends to be often used to refer only to fortunate outcomes, and the word has become more or less a synonym for 'lucky' or 'fortunate': *the ball went into the goal by a fortuitous ricochet*. Although this usage is now widespread, it is still regarded by some people as being rather informal and not correct.

founder, flounder

It is easy to confuse the words **founder** and **flounder**, not only because they sound similar but also because the contexts in which they are used tend to be similar. **Founder** means 'to fail', as in *the scheme foundered because of lack of organizational backing*. **Flounder**, on the other hand, means 'to be in difficulties', as in *new recruits floundering about in their first week.*

fragmentary

Fragmentary should be pronounced with the emphasis on the first syllable: /**frag**-muhn-tri/.

free rein

The image behind the phrase **give free rein** (to somebody) is from horse-riding, and the **rein** referred to is the strip of leather used to control a horse's (or child's) movements. Nowadays the spelling **free reign**, with an image taken from kingship, is almost as frequent, particularly in the US. In the Oxford English Corpus, 46 per cent of examples have the second spelling. Nevertheless, many people would consider the first spelling correct. For more information, see FOLK ETYMOLOGY.

-ful

The combining form **-ful** is used to form nouns meaning 'the amount needed to fill' (**cupful**, **spoonful**, etc.). The plural of such words is **cupfuls**, **spoonfuls**, etc., with the words joined together. *Three cups full* would mean the individual cups rather than a quantity measured in cups: *on the sill were three cups full of milk*, but *add three cupfuls of milk to the batter*.

fulsome

The modern, generally accepted meaning of **fulsome** is 'excessively complimentary or flattering' as in *a long and fulsome forty-seven page dedication to Princess Caroline*, but it is also often used to mean simply 'abundant', especially in uses such as *the critics have been fulsome in their praise*. Although this is in line with its earliest use, first recorded in the 13th century, some people consider it to be incorrect.

fun

The use of **fun** as an adjective meaning 'enjoyable', as in *we had a fun evening*, is not fully accepted in standard English and should only be used in informal contexts. There are signs that this situation is changing, though, given the recent appearance in US English of the comparative and superlative forms **funner** and **funnest**, formed as if **fun** were a normal adjective.

further, furthest

In some contexts **further** and **farther** are completely interchangeable: *she moved further/farther down the train*. The two words share the same roots and are equally correct when the meaning is 'at, to, or by a greater distance'. **Further** is a much commoner word, though, and is used in various abstract and metaphorical contexts, for example referring to time, where it would be unusual to use **farther**, e.g. *without further delay*; *have you anything further to say?*; *we intend to stay a further two weeks*. The same distinction is made between **farthest** and **furthest**: *the farthest point from the sun*, but: *this first team has gone furthest in its analysis*.

gay

Gay meaning 'homosexual' became established in the 1960s as the word preferred by homosexual men to describe themselves. It is now the standard accepted term throughout the English-speaking world. As a result, the centuries-old other meanings of **gay** meaning either 'carefree' or 'bright and showy' have more or less dropped out of natural use. The word **gay** cannot be readily used unselfconsciously today in these older meanings without suggesting a double entendre. **Gay** in its modern use typically refers to men, **lesbian** being the standard word for homosexual women, as in *the owners of a gay and lesbian bookstore*, but in some contexts it can be used of both men and women.

gender

The word **gender** has been used since the 14th century primarily as a grammatical term, referring to the classes of noun designated as masculine, feminine, or neuter in Latin, Greek, German, and other languages. It has also been used for just as long to refer to 'the state of being male or female', but this did not become a common standard use until the mid 20th century. Although the words **gender** and **sex** both mean 'the state of being male or female', they are typically used in slightly different ways: **sex** tends to refer to biological differences, while **gender** tends to refer to cultural or social ones.

gender-neutral language

In English, gender is explicit in nouns which refer exclusively to males or females, such as *businessman* and *actress*, and in the third person singular personal pronouns and adjectives *he*, *she*, *it*, *his*, *hers*, *its*, etc. Nowadays it is often very important to use language which implicitly or explicitly includes both men and women and makes no distinction between them. For more information on how to do this with nouns, see SEXIST LANGUAGE. What follows here is a discussion of how to be gender-neutral as regards pronouns such as *he* and determiners such as *his*.

1 From earliest times until about the 1960s people unquestioningly used the pronoun *he* (and *him*, *himself*, and *his*) when talking in general about one or more people of either sex. This most often happened:

- after indefinite pronouns and determiners such as *anybody*, *anyone*, *each*, *every*, etc., e.g. *anybody who really sets his heart on it*;
- after gender-neutral nouns such as *person*, *individual*, *speaker*, *student*, *researcher*, etc., e.g. *a researcher has to be completely objective in his findings*;
- in fixed expressions such as *every man for himself*.

2 Thanks to the feminist movement most people are now much more sensitive in these areas of language, ▶

and there are alternative ways of expressing these same ideas.

- When a gender-neutral pronoun is needed, the options usually adopted are *he or she* (or *his or her*, etc.), or the plural forms *they, their, themselves*. etc.
- Using *he or she*, etc., can be rather cumbersome, as in *each client should take the advice of his or her estate agent*, so there is a preference for using the plural form: *each client should take the advice of their estate agent*. Similarly *anyone who involves himself or herself in such issues does so for his or her own sake* is rather long-winded and better as *anyone who involves themselves in such issues does so for their own sake*.
- This use of plural pronouns following a singular subject is not new, but a revival of a practice dating from the 16th century. Nevertheless, some people object to it as ungrammatical. If you want to avoid it, an alternative strategy is to rephrase the sentence, generally by couching the whole thing in the plural. Recast in this way, the first example above becomes *clients should take the advice of their estate agents*.

3 Artificial devices, including the use of composite forms such as *s/he, hesh, wself*, etc., have not found general currency, partly because they are only possible in writing. A reflexive pronoun *themself* is occasionally used. This may become more common, but at present it is non-standard: *it is not an actor pretending to be Reagan or Thatcher, it is, in grotesque form, the person themself; someone in a neutral mood can devote themself solely to problem-solving*.

g

genealogy

The correct spelling is with the letter **a** before the ending **-logy**. Because most nouns referring to a branch of study end in **-ology**—*astrology, sociology*, etc.—people often write and say **geneology**, but this is incorrect.

genius

Genius used to be exclusively a noun, but is now quite often used as a sort of adjective: *I think it's a genius idea*. This use still has a tang of slang about it, and is best avoided in more formal writing.

geriatric

Geriatric is the normal, semi-official term used in Britain and the US when referring to the health care of old people (*a geriatric ward; geriatric patients*). When used outside such contexts, it typically carries overtones of being worn out and decrepit and can therefore be offensive if used to refer to people, as in *the photographer's bemused, bright-colour studies of the geriatric residents of San City*. In fact it may be seen as insulting to old people if used of anything else, e.g. *the US is full of geriatric coal-fired power stations*.

get

The verb **get** is one of the most common verbs in the English language. Nevertheless, despite its high frequency, there is still a feeling that almost any use containing **get** is somewhat informal. This may stem from the fact that many people were told at school not to write **get** at all, even though that was really only justifiable in relation to informal uses such as *I got a bike for my birthday*, and not standard expressions such as *he fought to get his breath back*.

girl

Few words are capable of raising some women's hackles as much as **girl** when used to refer to an adult woman. Conservatives may say that using it in this way is usually harmless and jokey; feminists might argue, in contrast, that it is disempowering and infantilizes women. It is certainly true that there is often a huge difference between the connotations of **girl** and those of **boy** when applied to adults: *his boyish charm* vs. *the film is a bit girlie*; *boys will be boys* vs. *he's a big girl's blouse*.

Since it is such a contentious word, it is better to be extremely cautious about making use of it.

Avoid using nouns which include it, such as *newsgirl*, *weathergirl*, *working girl*, *girl Friday*, and *career girl*, ▶

and use a neutral word: *newsreader*, *weather forecaster*, *working woman* or *sex worker*, *office assistant*, and *working woman* or *professional woman*.

Avoid using it to refer to any woman in a job or role, for instance *the woman who helps us out in the shop* rather than *the girl ...*

Although the word is still used informally by some women to refer to exclusive groups of women (*a night out with the girls*; *Come on girls! Let's show them we are more than cheerleaders with sticks*), not all women are happy with this use of it.

The one area where it still seems to be used consistently is in the popular press, in expressions such as *glamour girl*, *page-three girl*, *cover girl*, and so forth.

g

given name

See CHRISTIAN NAME.

glamorous

Both **glamor** and **glamour** are acceptable spellings in US English, but only the second is standard in British English, and is much commoner even in the US. Some people mistakenly suppose that **glamorous**, dropping the **u**, is an American spelling only. In fact, it is the correct spelling on both sides of the 'pond', while **glamourous** is universally a mistake. See also HUMOROUS.

Google

When referring to the Internet search engine itself, or the organization that owns it, **Google** should be written with a capital **G**. As a noun the name is a registered trademark, as a verb it is not. So, when using the word as a verb, you should write it with a small first letter: *I was idly googling two of my favourite words*. In that respect, you can treat it exactly like other verbs derived from trademarks, such as *to hoover* and *to xerox*.

gotten

Gotten and **got**, the past participles of **get**, both date back to Middle English. The form **gotten** is not generally used in British English but is very common in North American English, though even there it is often regarded as non-standard. In North American English, **got** and **gotten** are not identical in use. **Gotten** usually implies the process of obtaining something, as in *he had gotten us tickets for the show*, while **got** implies the state of possession or ownership, as in *I haven't got any money*. **Gotten** is also used in the meaning of 'become', as in *she's gotten very fat this last year.*

gourmand

The words **gourmand** and **gourmet** are similar but not identical in meaning. Both can be used to mean 'a connoisseur of good food' but **gourmand** is more usually used to mean 'a person who enjoys eating and often eats too much'. In other words, there is a hierarchy of finesse: *I am a gourmet, you are a gourmand, he is a glutton.*

graduate

The original use of this verb is **be graduated from**, i.e. as a transitive verb, used passively: *she will be graduated from medical school in June*. However, it is now much more common to say **graduate from**: *she will graduate from medical school in June*. A different transitive use, as in *he graduated high school last week*, is becoming increasingly common, especially in speech, but is considered incorrect by many editors.

graffiti

The word **graffiti** comes from Italian, and in Italian is a plural noun which has a singular form **graffito**. Traditionally, the same distinction was maintained in English, so that **graffiti** was used with a plural verb: *the graffiti were all over the wall*. Similarly, the singular would require a singular verb: *there was a graffito on the wall*. Today, this distinction survives in some specialist fields such as archaeology but sounds odd to most native speakers. The most common modern use is to treat **graffiti** as a singular and not to use **graffito** at all. In this case, **graffiti** takes a singular verb, as in *the graffiti was all over the wall*. Such uses are now widely accepted as standard, and may be regarded as part of the natural development of the language, rather than as mistakes. For more information, see NOUNS, SINGULAR AND PLURAL.

Great Britain

g

See BRITAIN.

grievous

This word has two syllables, /**gree**-vuhss/, and should not be pronounced as if it had three, /**gree**-vee-uhss/, since there is no letter **i** after the **v**.

grisly, grizzly

The words **grisly** and **grizzly** are quite different in meaning, though often confused. **Grisly** means 'gruesome', as in *grisly crimes*, whereas **grizzly** chiefly describes a kind of large American bear, but can also mean 'grey or grey-haired'.

grow

Although **grow** is typically used intransitively, as in *he would watch Nick grow to manhood*, using it as a transitive verb has long been standard in contexts which refer to growing plants and one's hair (*more land was needed to grow crops*; *she grew her hair long*). Recently, however, **grow** in its transitive meaning has become popular in business jargon: *entrepreneurs who are struggling to grow their businesses*. This is still a relatively new usage, and it is perhaps better to avoid it in formal contexts. It irritates certain people beyond measure.

gymnasium

The preferred plural form for this is **gymnasiums**. See also LATIN PLURALS.

h

Pronouncing the letter **h** at the beginning of words like *house, home,* and so on, has long been regarded as a yardstick of correct pronunciation in standard British English. Not pronouncing it, known as *dropping one's aitches*, is, conversely, considered to mark the speaker as regional or uneducated. So, it seems like a strange paradox that the exact opposite applies to how the letter itself is said. To pronounce it **aitch** is considered standard; to pronounce it **haitch**, non-standard (though it is the usual pronunciation in certain parts of the United Kingdom). But things have changed. While many people still regard the **haitch** pronunciation as anathema, it seems to be rapidly becoming the normal pronunciation for younger people, and carries no social stigma as far as they are concerned.

halcyon

The phrase **halcyon days**, referring to an idyllically happy period of time, is occasionally incorrectly turned into 'halcyonic days'.

half

People are sometimes not sure whether to use a singular or plural verb in phrases with **half**. When **half** is followed by a singular noun (with or without *of* between), the verb is also singular, and when the noun is plural the verb is plural: *half of the country is employed in agriculture*; *half the people like the idea*; *half that amount is enough*. Occasionally, when **half (of)** is used with a collective noun, the plural can correctly be used: *nearly half (of) the population lose at least half their teeth before they reach the age of 40*.

handicapped

The word **handicapped** is first recorded in the early 20th century to refer to a person's mental or physical disabilities. In British English it was the standard term until relatively recently, but like many terms in this sensitive field its prominence has been short-lived. It has been superseded by more recent terms such as **disabled**, or, when referring to mental disability, **having**

learning difficulties or **learning-disabled**. In American English, however, **handicapped** remains acceptable.

hang

In modern English **hang** has two past tense and past participle forms: **hanged** and **hung**. **Hung** is the normal form in most general uses, e.g. *they hung out the washing*; *she hung around for a few minutes*; *he had hung the picture over the fireplace*, but **hanged** is the normal form to refer to execution by hanging: *the prisoner was hanged*. The reason for this distinction is a complex historical one: **hanged**, the earlier form, was superseded by **hung** sometime after the 16th century; it is likely that the retention of **hanged** for the execution meaning has to do with the tendency of archaic forms to live on in the legal language of the courts.

harass

There are two possible pronunciations of the word **harass**: one emphasizing the first syllable, /**ha**-ruhs/, and the other, the second: /huh-**ras**/. /**Ha**-ruhs/ is the older one and is regarded by some people as the only correct one, especially in British English. However, the pronunciation /huh-**ras**/ is very common and is now accepted as a standard alternative.

hardly

1 Words such as **hardly**, **scarcely**, and **rarely** should not be used with negative constructions. It is correct to say *I can hardly wait* but incorrect to say *I can't hardly wait*. This is because adverbs such as **hardly** are treated as if they were negatives, and it is a grammatical rule of standard English that double negatives (i.e. in this case having **hardly** and **not** in the same clause) are not acceptable. Words such as **hardly** behave as negatives in other respects as well, as for example in combining with words such as **any** or **at all**, which are normally only used where a negative is present: standard usage is *I've got hardly any money*.

2 See also DOUBLE NEGATIVE.

harelip

Use of the word **harelip** can cause offence and should be avoided; use **cleft lip** instead.

hash

In British English this is the normal name for the symbol #, for example on a telephone keypad. In the US and elsewhere it is called either the **number sign**, in contexts such as *question #2*; or the **pound sign**, on telephone keypads or when used as a symbol for pounds of weight, e.g. *2# of sugar*. You may impress your friends briefly by telling them that the technical name for this symbol is the **octothorp**, but that name is not widely used.

hashtag

This refers to the use of the hash symbol # in front of a word or phrase on social media sites such as Twitter, to identify messages on a specific topic.

have

1 **Have** and **have got**: there is a great deal of debate on the difference between these two forms. A traditional view is that **have got** is chiefly British, but not correct in formal writing, while **have** is chiefly American. Actual usage is more complicated: **have got** is in fact also widely used in US English. In both British and US usage **have** is more formal than **have got** and it is more appropriate in writing to use constructions such as **do not have** rather than **have not got**.

2 A common mistake is to write the word **of** instead of **have** or **'ve**: *I could of told you that* instead of *I could have told you that*. The reason for the mistake is that the pronunciation of **have** in unstressed contexts is the same as that of **of**, and people confuse the two in writing. The error was recorded as early as 1837 and, though common, is unacceptable in standard English.

3 Another controversial issue is the insertion of an unnecessary **have** referring to a hypothetical situation introduced by **if**, as for example *I might have missed it if you hadn't* ***have*** *pointed it out* (rather than the standard ... *if you hadn't pointed it out*). This construction has been around since at least the

15th century, and there has recently been speculation among grammarians and linguists that it may represent a kind of subjunctive and is actually making a useful distinction in the language. However, it is still regarded as an error in standard English.

he

1 For a discussion of *I am older than he* versus *I am older than him*, see PERSONAL PRONOUN.

2 At one time, **he** was used uncontroversially to refer to a person of unspecified sex, as in *every child needs to know that* ***he*** *is loved*. Nowadays, this use has become problematic and is a hallmark of old-fashioned or sexist language. **They** as an alternative to **he** (*everyone needs to feel that* ***they*** *matter*) has been in use since the 18th century, in contexts where it occurs after an indefinite pronoun such as **everyone** or **someone**. Despite objections by some, it is now widely accepted both in speech and in writing. Another alternative is **he or she**, but this can become tiresomely long-winded when used frequently. See also GENDER-NEUTRAL LANGUAGE.

her

For a discussion of *I am older than her* versus *I am older than she*, or *it's her all right* rather than *it's she all right*, see PERSONAL PRONOUN.

hers

There is no need for an apostrophe: the spelling should be **hers** not **her's**.

him

For a discussion of *I could never be as good as him* versus *I could never be as good as he*, see PERSONAL PRONOUN.

Hindustani

Hindustani was the usual term in the 18th and 19th centuries for the native language of NW India. The usual modern term is

Hindi (or **Urdu** in Muslim contexts), although **Hindustani** is still used to refer to the dialect of Hindi spoken around Delhi.

Hispanic

In the US **Hispanic** is the standard accepted term when referring to Spanish-speaking people living in the US. Other, more specific, terms such as **Latino** and **Chicano** are also used where occasion demands.

historic, historical

1 On the use of *an historic moment* or *a historic moment*, see AN.

2 **Historic** and **historical** are used in slightly different ways. **Historic** means 'famous or important in history', as in *a(n) historic occasion*, whereas **historical** means 'concerning history or historical events', as in *historical evidence*. An *historic event* is one that was very important, whereas an *historical event* is something that happened in the past. Confusing the two is something careful writers avoid.

hoard

The words **hoard** and **horde** are similar in meaning and are pronounced the same, and so they are sometimes confused. A **hoard** is 'a secret stock or store of something', as in *a hoard of treasure*, while a **horde** is sometimes a disparaging word for 'a large group of people', as in *hordes of fans descended on the stage*. Instances of **hoard** being used instead of **horde** are not uncommon: around 10 per cent of the uses of **hoard** in the Oxford English Corpus are incorrect.

hoi polloi

1 **Hoi** is one of the Greek words for the definite article *the*; the phrase **hoi polloi** thus translates as 'the many'. This knowledge has led some traditionalists to insist that it should not be used in English with *the*, since that would be to state the word *the* twice. However, the fact is that, once established in English, expressions such as **hoi polloi** are treated as a fixed unit and are subject to the rules and conventions of English. Evidence shows that use with *the* has now become an accepted part of standard English usage.

2 **Hoi polloi** is sometimes used to mean 'upper class', i.e. the exact opposite of its normal meaning. This is not recommended, for the obvious reason that you could be completely misunderstood.

home in, hone in

If you **home in on** something you focus all your attention on it: *we've homed in on the products that are most sought after*. For some reason, people very often say and write **hone in on** to express this meaning. **Hone** may become a perfectly acceptable variant in future; for the time being, it is still generally considered a mistake.

homogeneous

This word meaning 'uniform, alike' is correctly spelled **homogeneous** with an **e** before the **ou**, and pronounced /hom-uh-**jee**-ni-uhs/, but it is frequently spelled **homogenous** and pronounced /huh-**mo**-ji-nuhs/. This rarely matters, but it is good to be aware that **homogenous** is a different word, an albeit dated term used in biology.

hopefully

The traditional meaning of **hopefully**, 'in a hopeful manner', has been in use since the 17th century. In the second half of the 20th century a new use, commenting on the whole sentence, arose, meaning 'it is to be hoped that', as in *hopefully, we'll see you tomorrow*. This second use is now very much commoner than the first use, but it is still widely believed to be incorrect. This is somewhat illogical. People do not criticize other similar adverbs, e.g. **sadly** (as in *sadly, her father died last year*) or **fortunately** (as in *fortunately, he recovered*). Part of the reason is that **hopefully** is a rather odd adverb of this kind: while many others, such as **sadly**, **regrettably**, and **clearly**, may be paraphrased as 'it is sad/regrettable/clear that . . . ', this is not possible with **hopefully**. Nevertheless, it is clear that use of **hopefully** has become a test case of 'correctness' in the language—even if the arguments on which this is based are not particularly strong—and it may be wise to avoid its use in formal or written contexts.

horde

The words **hoard** and **horde** are quite distinct; see HOARD.

hotel

The normal pronunciation of **hotel** sounds the **h-**, which means that you should write and say *a hotel*. However, the older pronunciation without the **h-** is still sometimes heard, in which case *an hotel* would be appropriate. For a discussion of this, see AN.

Hottentot

Hottentot is first recorded in the late 17th century and was a name applied by white Europeans to the Khoikhoi group of peoples of South Africa and Namibia. It is now regarded as offensive when referring to people and should always be avoided in favour of **Khoikhoi** or the names of the particular peoples, such as the Nama. The only acceptable modern use for **Hottentot** is in the names of animals and plants, such as the *Hottentot cherry*.

however, how ever

If you use **ever** for emphasis after **how** or **why**, you should write it as a separate word. It is correct to write *how ever did you manage*? rather than *however did you manage*? In contrast, **however** is written as one word in the following cases: when it is equivalent to 'but' (*when the film opened in 1923, however, audiences stayed away in droves*); when it means 'in whatever way' (*take that however you like*); and when it means 'to whatever extent' (*he is exempt from any rule , however clearly stated it is*). But, with other words such as **what**, **where**, and **who**, the situation is not clear-cut: people write both **what ever** and **whatever**, and so on, and neither is regarded as particularly more correct than the other.

humanitarian

Humanitarian means 'concerned with or seeking to promote human welfare', so it is rather loosely used in sentences such as *this is the worst humanitarian disaster this country has seen*, where it just means 'human'. This use is quite common, especially in journalism, but is not generally considered good style.

humankind

Humankind is often used as a non-sexist replacement for **mankind**. See also MAN.

h

humorous

Though **humor** is the standard US spelling for British **humour**, it is a mistake to suppose that only Americans write **humorous**. It is the correct spelling on both sides of the Atlantic, while **humourous** is a mistake everywhere. See also GLAMOROUS.

hypercorrection

Hypercorrection is an incorrect use of language because, in an attempt to be correct, one is following a rule that does not apply. There are common hypercorrect forms in the areas of grammar, spelling, and pronunciation.

- A grammatical example is *between you and I*, instead of the correct *between you and me*, caused by people's belief that *you and me* is always wrong, not just as the subject of a sentence, as in *you and me could go to the cinema*.
- *Glamourous* is a hypercorrect spelling, based on the belief that because *glamor* is the US spelling equivalent to the British *glamour*, *glamorous* must be a US spelling too.
- Hypercorrect pronunciations are very often of foreign words, for instance that of pronouncing *machismo* with -k- in the middle, thinking that -ch- is too English a sound to be in a foreign word.

hyphenation

Hyphenation is an area in which practice is somewhat fluid, since it varies between different types of English and different house styles, and evolves over time. As H. W. Fowler wrote in his *Modern English Usage* (1926): '. . . its infinite variety defies description'. He did, however, also say that the hyphen 'is not an ornament but an aid to being understood', and that laudable aim often governs its use, as illustrated below.

The primary function of the hyphen is to indicate that two or more words should be interpreted together as a single unit of meaning, and the examples below use that as the basis to show why it is necessary in some cases and unnecessary in others. There are also cases where its use varies according to context. Nouns are dealt with separately, since they raise questions of their own.

Necessary uses

- in many, but not all, compound adjectives of various sorts, e.g. (noun + adjective) *accident-prone, sports-mad, sugar-free, carbon-neutral, time-poor, camera-ready*; (noun/adjective + participle) *computer-aided, custom-built, good-looking, quick-thinking, slow-moving*; (noun + ing/ed) *stress-busting, muddle-headed*; (adjective + noun (+ ed)) *seventh-century, double-breasted, short-sighted*. NB: it is important to use hyphens in adjectives referring to ages and durations, since leaving them out can create ambiguity: compare *250-year-old trees* and *250 year old trees*; in the second the trees could be merely a year old.
- in compound adjectives formed from adverb + past participle, e.g. *well-equipped*, and in adjectives based on phrases, e.g. *in-your-face, top-of-the-range*, which are hyphenated when they come before the noun but ▶

not when they follow it: *this is a top-of-the-range model*, but *this model is top of the range*.

- in many verbs formed from nouns: *they booby-trapped the door; he was body-searched*
- to separate certain prefixes, especially those derived from classical languages, e.g. *anti-intellectual*, *co-driver*, *ex-directory*, *extra-large*, *over-intellectual*, *pro-life*, *post-coital*

  NB: in American usage, words in the last group are often written without a hyphen.

- to separate pairs of vowels or consonants which could otherwise be misread or sound awkward: *co-opt* (*coopt* could be read as /koopt/), *pre-eminent* (which could look like preem-), *drip-proof*
- to distinguish *re-cover* (= 'cover again') from *recover*; *re-sort* (= 'sort again') from *resort*, etc.
- to separate a prefix from a name, designation, or date: *post-Aristotelian*; *ex-husband*; *pre-1960s*
- with *odd* when used with a number, e.g. *thirty-odd people* ('approximately thirty people'), as opposed to *thirty odd people* ('thirty people who are odd').

Use varies according to context

As noted above, if an adjective such as *top-of-the-range* or *up-to-date* comes before the noun it is hyphenated, but otherwise it is not: *an up-to-date account*, but *I like to keep up to date*.

Mid in compounds before nouns is hyphenated, e.g. *a mid-nineteenth century forgery*, but otherwise it functions as an adjective in its own right and is not hyphenated, e.g. *in the mid nineteenth century*.

The suffixes *-less* and *-like* need a hyphen if the root word ends with *-ll*: *cell-less*, *thrill-less*, *doll-like*, *shell-like*.

Unnecessary uses

Hyphens are superfluous in:

- phrasal verbs: *to give up the fight*, not *to give-up the fight*
- adjective phrases formed from an adverb ending in *-ly* and a participle, as in *a poorly understood condition* ▶

(not poorly-understood), *a widely held view* (not a widely-held view)

Nouns

Compound nouns consisting of two words can in principle be written in one of three different ways: e.g. *air fare*, *air-fare*, or *airfare*. In practice, however, the use of hyphens in compound nouns is generally decreasing. Usage in the US tends towards writing the two nouns as one, and usage in Britain tends towards writing them separately, as is the case with *air fare* etc. Otherwise there are few hard-and-fast rules, but a few tendencies can be detected, e.g.:

- Compounds of which the first element has only one syllable are some of the most likely to be written as one word, e.g. *website*, *spyware*, *blockbuster*, *playgroup*, as opposed to *bottle bank*, *filling station*, *regime change*.
- If the first element is an adjective, the compound tends to stay as separate words, e.g. *virtual reality*, *black box*.
- Compounds tend to stay as two words if joining them up would produce an awkward or misleading result, as with *wood duck*, *binge drinker*.
- Hyphens are used in well-established multiword nouns, such as *stick-in-the-mud*, *ne'er-do-well*, *jack-in-the-box*.
- They are also used with most nouns derived from phrasal verbs, such as *build-up*, *warm-up*, *carry-on*, *walk-through*. A few very common ones are written predominantly as one word, e.g. *handout*, *breakthrough*, *pickup*, but usage varies a great deal.

I

It is incorrect to say *between you and I* instead of *between you and me*. See BETWEEN. It is also incorrect to say *John and me went to the shops* instead of *John and I went to the shops*. On this point and whether it is correct to say *she's much better than me* or *she's much better than I*, see PERSONAL PRONOUN.

-i

Many nouns that are derived from a foreign language retain their foreign plural, at least when they first enter English and particularly if they belong to a specialist field. Over time, however, it is quite normal for a word in general use to acquire a regular English plural. This regular plural may coexist with the foreign plural (e.g. **cactus**, plural **cactuses** or **cacti**) or, more commonly, especially over time, oust it (e.g. **octopus**, plural **octopuses** rather than **octopodes**). The plural ending **-i** is more persistent that many other foreign plural endings, probably because it is a better-known one—so well known, in fact, that it is sometimes applied to words which never had it in the first place, as with the spurious *octopi*.

if

If and **whether** are more or less interchangeable in sentences like *I'll see if he left an address* and *I'll see whether he left an address*, although **whether** is generally regarded as more formal and suitable for written use.

ignoramus

The correct plural of **ignoramus** is **ignoramuses**. This may sound odd, considering the word is from Latin, leading one to think the plural ought to be *'ignorami'*. However, it was never a noun in Latin, only a verb, meaning literally 'we do not know', and the English word derives from the name of a character in George Ruggle's play *Ignoramus* (1615), a satirical comedy exposing lawyers' ignorance. For more information on the plural forms of Latin words, see LATIN PLURALS.

ilk

Nowadays, **ilk** is used in phrases such as *of his ilk*, *of that ilk*, to mean 'type' or 'sort'. This use arose out of a misunderstanding of the earlier, Scottish use in the phrase **of that ilk**, where it means 'of the same name or place'. For this reason, some traditionalists regard the modern use as incorrect. It is, however, the only common current use and is now part of standard English.

illegal, illicit

Something that is **illegal** is against the law, as in *illegal drugs, illegal immigrants*. **Illicit** traditionally covers things that are forbidden or disapproved of but not against the law, as in *an illicit love affair*, but it is commonly used to mean the same as **illegal**.

imminent

For the mistaken use of **eminent** to mean **imminent**, see EMINENT.

impact

The verb **impact on**, as in *when produce is lost, it always impacts on the bottom line*, has been in the language since the 1960s. Many people disapprove of it, despite its relative frequency, saying that **make an impact on** or other equivalent wordings should be used instead. They may object partly because new forms of verbs from nouns (as in the case of **impact**) are often regarded as somehow inferior. Also, since the use of **impact** is associated with business and commercial writing, it has the unenviable status of jargon, which makes it doubly disliked. For further information, see VERBS FORMED FROM NOUNS.

imply

Imply and **infer** do not mean the same thing and are not interchangeable: see INFER.

important, importantly

Both **more/most important** and **more/most importantly** are used as written asides, e.g. *a non-drinking, non-smoking, and, more importantly, non-political sportsman*. It is sometimes maintained that the only correct form in this use is **important**, on the grounds that it stands for 'what is more/most important'. However, **importantly** used in this way is perfectly well established and acceptable in modern English.

impracticable, impractical

Although their meanings are similar, **impracticable** and **impractical** should not be used in exactly the same way.

Impracticable means 'impossible to carry out' and is normally used of a specific procedure or course of action, as in *poor visibility made the task difficult, even impracticable*. **Impractical**, on the other hand, tends to be used in a more general way, often to mean simply 'unrealistic' or 'not sensible': *in windy weather an umbrella is impractical*. It is good style to avoid using **impracticable** in such contexts.

improvise

Improvise is always spelled *-ise* not *-ize*.

include

i

Include has a broader meaning than **comprise**. In the sentence *the accommodation comprises 2 bedrooms, bathroom, kitchen, and living room*, the word **comprise** implies that there is no accommodation other than that listed. **Include** can be used in this way too, but it is also used in a less restrictive way, implying that there may be other things not specifically mentioned that are part of the same category, as in *the price includes a special welcome pack*.

Indian

The native peoples of America came to be described as **Indian** as a result of Christopher Columbus and other voyagers in the 15th and 16th centuries believing that, when they reached the east coast of America, they had reached part of India by a new route. The terms **Indian** and **Red Indian** are today regarded as old-fashioned and inappropriate, recalling, as they do, the stereotypical portraits of the Wild West. **American Indian**, however, is well established. See also AMERICAN INDIAN and NATIVE AMERICAN.

Indigenous Australians

See ABORIGINAL, ABORIGINE.

infectious

On the differences in meaning between **infectious** and **contagious**, see CONTAGIOUS.

infer

Infer and **imply** mean different things. In the sentence *the speaker implied that the General had been a traitor*, **implied** means that something in the speaker's words **suggested** that this man was a traitor (though nothing so explicit was actually stated). However, in *we inferred from his words that the General had been a traitor*, **inferred** means that something in the speaker's words enabled us to **deduce** that the man was a traitor. So, the two words **infer** and **imply** can describe the same event, but from different angles. Mistakes occur when **infer** is used to mean **imply**, as in *are you inferring that I'm a liar?* (instead of *are you implying that I'm a liar?*). The error is so common that some dictionaries record it as a more or less standard use: over 20 per cent of examples for **infer** in the Oxford English Corpus are a mistaken replacement for **imply**. Nevertheless, many people still regard the use of **infer** for **imply** as an error.

inflammable

The words **inflammable** and **flammable** mean the same thing, 'easily set on fire'. This may seem surprising, since the prefix **in**- normally negates the adjective that follows it, as in *indirect* and *insufficient*, so you might expect **inflammable** to mean the opposite of **flammable**, i.e. 'not easily set on fire'. The reason that it means the same as **flammable** is that **inflammable** is formed using a different Latin prefix **in**-, which means 'into' and here has the effect of intensifying the meaning. **Flammable** is a far commoner word than **inflammable** and is less likely to confuse people.

innit

The word **innit** arose as an informal way of saying 'isn't it', especially in questions in spoken English where the speaker is seeking confirmation of a statement, as in *weird that, innit?* More recently, however, **innit** has also started serving as *don't I?*, *can't you?*, *aren't we?*, etc., either when there is a genuine seeking of confirmation or merely for emphasis, as in *we're all friends, innit?* This extended use is especially common among young people and is often satirized. (Interestingly, many other languages have just one expression equivalent to all these English ones: *n'est-ce pas?* in French, for example, or *nicht wahr?* in German.) From this confirmation-seeking or emphatic use, **innit** has further developed into a general-purpose 'filler', conveying very little actual content, as in *some MCs just MC but they don't really know what's going on, on the road innit... but we know innit*. In this type of context, it is much like *you know* or *sort of*.

input

As a verb, **input** has the past tense and past participle **input** and **inputted**, both of which are correct, though **input** is more often used. See also VERBS FORMED FROM NOUNS.

i

inquire

On the difference between **inquire** and **enquire**, see ENQUIRE.

insurance

There is a technical distinction between **insurance** and **assurance** in the context of life insurance: see ASSURANCE.

insure

Insure and **ensure** are related in meaning and use. In both British and US English the main meaning of **insure** is the commercial meaning of providing financial compensation in the event of damage to property; **ensure** is not used at all with this meaning. For the more general meaning of 'to make sure', **ensure that** is at least 50 times more common in the Oxford English Corpus than **insure that**, as in *the system is run to ensure that a good quality of service is maintained*. In similar examples to the last one, **insure that** is sometimes used but is likely to be regarded as a mistake.

integral

There are two possible pronunciations for **integral** as an adjective: /**in**-ti-gruhl/ and /in-**teg**-ruhl/. /In-**teg**-ruhl/ is sometimes frowned on, but both are acceptable as standard.

intense, intensive

Intense and **intensive** are similar in meaning, but they differ in emphasis. **Intense** tends to relate to subjective responses—emotions and how we feel about something—while **intensive**, in the meaning of 'very thorough, vigorous', tends to be an objective description. So, *an intensive course* simply describes the type of course: one that is designed to cover a lot of ground in a short time. On the other hand, in *the course was intense*, **intense** describes how someone felt about the course. *Intense negotiations* are ones where there is a lot of tension and emotional excitement, while *intensive negotiations* are very thorough and probably concentrated into a short period of time. **Intensive** is sometimes used where **intense** is meant, as in *an intensive love of Tolkien*, but this should be avoided in writing.

i

interface

The word **interface** has existed as a noun since the 1880s. The metaphorical meaning, 'a place or means of interactions between two systems, organizations, etc.', to which many people object, was first used before the literal, computing meaning. It has become widespread in this extended use as both a noun and a verb in all sorts of spheres. Some people object to it on the grounds that there are plenty of other words that could be used instead. Although it is now well established as a part of standard English, if you wish to avoid it in certain contexts you could use *interaction*, *liaison*, *dialogue*, *contact*, etc., and their related verbs. See also VERBS FORMED FROM NOUNS.

in terms of

In terms of is to be treated with extreme caution. Widely criticized for being overused and vague, it is often abused as an all-purpose way of cobbling together fuzzy ideas, as this example from the business world illustrates: *the effect would be significant in terms of potential impact on earnings*. The problem with this sentence is that it says the same thing twice. It should be cut down to size as *the effect on potential earnings would be* *significant*. And the same is true of many sentences where it is used as a connector like this. Assess any sentence in which you write it with a critical eye. Does it make your point easier to understand—or merely long-winded? **In terms of** is also often used at the start of a clause, to announce the topic: *there were also benefits in terms of reducing fixed costs, he said*. While it can be a useful hook on which to hang your thoughts when speaking, in writing preferable alternatives for this use are **as for**, **as regards**, or, more forcefully, **when it comes to**.

Inuit

i

The peoples living in the regions from the central Canadian Arctic to western Greenland prefer to be called **Inuit** rather than **Eskimo**, a broader term including peoples living elsewhere in the Arctic region, notably Siberia. **Inuit** now has official status in Canada. It is also used as a synonym for **Eskimo** in general, usually in an attempt to be politically correct, but is best avoided in that meaning, for the reason just mentioned. See also ESKIMO.

irregardless

Irregardless means the same as **regardless**, but the negative prefix **ir-** merely duplicates the suffix **-less**, and is completely unnecessary. The word dates back to the 19th century, and may be a confusion of **regardless** with **irrespective**. It is regarded as incorrect in standard English, and most people would regard it as a non-word.

-ise

There are some verbs which must be spelled **-ise** and are not variants of the **-ize** ending. Most reflect a French influence, and they include **advertise**, **compromise**, **enterprise**, **improvise**, and **televise**. For more details, see -IZE OR -ISE.

issue

Many people object to the overuse of the word **issue** referring to emotional and psychological difficulties, or to problems in providing a service: *emotions and intimacy issues that were largely dealt with through alcohol; a small number of users are experiencing* *connectivity issues*. In both contexts, the word is clearly a euphemism. In the first case, by avoiding the word **problem**, it casts the person concerned in a less negative light. However, in this use it often has an aura of psychobabble about it. In the second case, **issue** is meant to imply that a solution will be found, and that everything is under control. While the intention behind using the word in these ways may be praiseworthy, overuse has turned it into a cliché, beloved of politicians and pundits. If you want an alternative, you may have to call a spade a spade and use a word which is rapidly becoming taboo: **a problem**.

its

A common error in writing is to confuse the possessive **its** (as in *turn the camera on its side*) with the contraction **it's** (short for either **it is** or **it has**, as in *it's my fault*; *it's been a hot day*). The confusion is understandable since the possessive forms of singular nouns do take an apostrophe + **-s**, as in *the girl's bike*; *the President's smile*.

-ize or -ise

The main difficulties people encounter with words ending in **-ize** and **-ise** are:

- which words have alternative spellings and which don't?
- where there are alternative spellings, which is the correct one?

This article gives guidance on both these aspects, as well as commenting on some relatively recent words ending in *-ize*.

1 The reason there is a choice in many cases between *-ize* and *-ise* is historically complex. The *-ize* ending ultimately derives from the Classical Greek verbal ending *-izo*, whether or not the English verb existed in Greek in the same form. Many words with alternative endings in *-ize*/*-ise* have come to English via Latin and French sources, but in French the ▶

spelling has been adapted to *-ise*. The first *-ize* word recorded in English is *baptize*, from the 13th century. In French it is written *baptiser*, and a large proportion of English writers and publishers followed suit by writing the word as *baptise*.

2 There is a small group of words which are only ever written *-ise*, in all varieties of English, including American English, and they are listed below. It may help to remember that *-ise* is obligatory where it forms part of a larger word element, such as *-cise* in *excise*, *-mise* in *compromise*, *-prise* in *surprise*, and *-vise* in *supervise*. *-ise* is also obligatory in verbs closely related to nouns with **-s-** in the stem, such as *advertise* (compare *advertisement*) and *televise* (which is actually derived from *television*).

advertise
advise
apprise
arise
chastise
circumcise
comprise
compromise
demise
despise
devise
dis(en)franchise
disguise
enfranchise
enterprise
excise
exercise
franchise
improvise
incise
merchandise
prise (open)
reprise

▶

revise
supervise
surmise
surprise
televise

3 Words where there is a choice of ending such as *authorize/authorise*, *civilize/civilise*, *legalize/legalise* may be correctly spelled with either *-ize* or *-ise* throughout the English-speaking world, except in America, where *-ize* is always used.
In other cases the choice is a matter of house style. However, Oxford University Press and many other publishing houses prefer the spelling in *-ize*.
British English writers are generally aware of the choice but often mistakenly regard the *-ize* ending as an Americanism. They tend to be particularly reluctant to use the *-ize* form in words which have other forms in which the letter *s* features, such as *criticize* (*criticism*), *hypnotize* (*hypnosis*), and *emphasize* (*emphasis*).

4 Adding *-ize* to a noun or adjective has been a standard way of forming new verbs for centuries, and verbs such as *characterize*, *terrorize*, and *sterilize* were all formed in this way hundreds of years ago. For some reason some people object to recent formations of this type: during the 20th century, objections were raised against **prioritize**, **finalize**, and **hospitalize**, among others. There does not seem to be any coherent reason for such objections, except that verbs formed from nouns tend, in general and for no clear reason, to be criticized. Despite objections, it is clear that *-ize* forms are an accepted part of the standard language.

judgement

In British English the traditional spelling in general contexts is **judgement**, though **judgment** without the **-e-** is also often found. However, the spelling **judgment** is the standard spelling in legal contexts, and in all contexts in North American English.

Kaffir

The word **Kaffir** is first recorded in the 16th century (as **Caffre**) and was originally simply an innocuous descriptive term for a particular ethnic group. Although it survives in the names of a few plants, such as the *Kaffir lily*, it is always a racially abusive and offensive term when used of people, and in South Africa its use is actionable.

Khoikhoi

To refer to the indigenous peoples of Namibia and parts of South Africa, **Khoikhoi** should be used in preference to **Hottentot**, since the latter is likely to cause offence: see also HOTTENTOT.

kilometre (US kilometer)

There are two possible pronunciations for **kilometre**: /**kil**-uh-mee-tuh/ and /ki-**lom**-i-tuh/. The first is traditionally considered correct, with a stress pattern similar to other units of measurement such as *centimetre*. The second pronunciation, which originated in US English and is now also very common in British English, is still regarded as incorrect by some people, especially in British English.

kind

The use of **kind** sometimes causes difficulty, as in *these kind of questions are not relevant*, where the plurals *these* and *are* are used with the singular *kind*. With *this* or *that*, speaking of one kind, use a singular construction: ***this kind** of question **is** not relevant; **that kind** of fabric **doesn't** need ironing*. With *these* or *those*, speaking of more than one kind, use a plural construction: *we refuse to buy **these kinds** of books; I've given up **those kinds** of ideas*. The ungrammatical *these kind* has been used since the 14th century, but although often encountered today it should be avoided. The same point applies to the noun **sort** used in a similar way.

koala

Koalas, the bear-like Australian marsupials, are widely called **koala bears** in everyday language. Zoologists, however, regard this form as incorrect on the grounds that, despite appearances, koalas are completely unrelated to bears.

kudos

Kudos comes from Greek and means 'praise'. Despite appearances, it is not a plural word. This means that there is no singular form **kudo** and that the use of **kudos** as a plural, as in the following sentence, is incorrect: *he received many kudos for his work* (correct use is *he received much kudos for his work*).

Lapp

Although the word **Lapp** is still widely used and is the most familiar term to many people, the indigenous people referred to by this name consider it somewhat offensive: the better term to use is **Sami**. The name **Samiland** for the area they inhabit has yet to fully establish itself.

last, lastly

When introducing points or topics in sequence it is good style to be consistent in your choice of words. If you use **firstly**, **secondly**, and so on, **lastly** fits better than **last**. On the other hand, if you introduce your first point with **first**, **last** at the end is perfectly acceptable; see also FIRST.

Latin plurals

Many relatively common words in English have been borrowed directly from Latin. Sometimes their plurals are formed following English rules, by adding a letter **s**, and sometimes following Latin rules; often there are two different plural forms for the same word, as in *referendum*, *referendums/referenda*.

As a rule of thumb, the Latin-style plural is appropriate in scientific, technical, or very formal language, and the English plural in all other contexts. So, telling your friends about the different 'aquaria' you have visited (rather ▶

than the different 'aquariums') might make them titter or guffaw, whereas for a marine biologist to talk about 'aquaria' would be entirely fitting.

Plurals which are more common than their singular counterparts, such as *criteria* and *bacteria*, are frequently used with a singular meaning, as in *we didn't have a set criteria when we started working*. Such uses are not good style, and will be considered completely wrong by some people. The lists below show the different forms, and also highlight some common mistakes to avoid.

Forming plurals

SINGULAR	PLURAL
-um	**-ums** *or* **-a**
addendum	addendums or addenda
aquarium	aquariums or aquaria
crematorium	crematoriums or crematoria
gymnasium	gymnasiums or gymnasia
maximum	maximums or maxima
memorandum	memorandums or memoranda
minimum	minimums or minima
moratorium	moratoriums or moratoria
referendum	referendums or referenda

Most of the words above have both English-style and Latin-style plurals, and the guidance given earlier holds good. Note that *stratum* only has the plural *strata*.

SINGULAR	PLURAL
-us	**-uses**
bonus	bonuses
callus	calluses
caucus	caucuses
focus	focuses
f(o)etus	f(o)etuses
ignoramus	ignoramuses
lotus	lotuses
octopus	octopuses
phallus	phalluses

▶

prospectus	prospectuses
sinus	sinuses
surplus	surpluses
virus	viruses

For all of these, if you make the plural by adding **-es** you will not go wrong, and in many cases there is no plural in **-i**. In the Oxford English Corpus, *syllabi* is about twice as common as *syllabuses*, while *narcissi* is much preferred over *narcissuses*.

SINGULAR	PLURAL
-a	**-ae**
amoeba	amoebas
larva	larvae

Amoebae is often used in scientific writing, and *amoebas* more generally. The plural of *larva* is always *larvae* (**lar**-vee).

Antenna has alternative plural forms with different meanings: strictly speaking, an insect has *antennae*, while *antennas* are telecommunications aerials, although these are quite often called *antennae* as well.

Formulae traditionally come up in science and maths, and *formulas* are solutions to general problems. Though this distinction is often blurred, it is wise to stick to the first in scientific contexts.

SINGULAR	PLURAL
-x	**-xes** or **-ces**
apex	apexes or apices
appendix	appendixes or appendices
codex	codexes or codices
cortex	cortexes or cortices
crux	cruxes or cruces
helix	helixes or helices
index	indexes or indices
vortex	vortexes or vortices

As these words are mainly used in technical or scientific texts, the Latinate forms such as ▶

apices are commoner. Note that the plural of *crux* is generally *cruxes*.

Appendix and *index* have alternative plural forms with different meanings. *Appendixes* may require an operation, while *appendices* are to be found at the end of some books; following them you may find *indexes*, while *indices* measure things.

Watch out for:

Addenda, *bacteria*, *criteria*, *errata*, and *strata* are often used with a singular meaning, which is a mistake to avoid in writing. The correct forms are *addendum*, *bacterium*, *criterion*, *erratum*, and *stratum*.
Octopi and *ignorami* as plurals are grammatically mistaken, even though they sound authentic: *octopuses* and *ignoramuses* are correct.

latter

You should avoid using **latter** when mentioning more than two people or things. For an explanation, see FORMER.

lay

Some forms of the verb lay are often used instead of the appropriate forms of **lie**. For instance, it is incorrect to say: *why don't you lay on the bed* (the correct form is **lie**); *she was laying on the bed* (the correct form is **lying**). The form **laid**, the past participle of **lay**, is also quite often mistakenly used instead of **lain**, which is the correct past participle of **lie**. So, *he had* lain *on the floor for hours* is correct, while *he had* laid *on the floor on the floor...* is not. Finally, it is incorrect to use **lie** followed by an object, as in *she was lying her head on his shoulder*, where the correct use is *she was laying her head...*

layman

To avoid sounding unintentionally sexist you could consider replacing **layman** with **layperson** in the singular and **laypeople** in the plural: *in layperson's terms; scholars and educated laypeople alike.* See also MAN and SEXIST LANGUAGE.

lean

Though the forms **leant** and **leaned** for the past tense and past participle are equally acceptable, **leaned** is markedly more common in all varieties of English.

leap

Though the forms **leapt** and **leaped** for the past tense and past participle are equally acceptable, **leapt** is markedly more common in all varieties of English.

learn

Learn is one of the small group of verbs which have alternative forms for the past tense and past participle. Usage varies according to the variety of English you speak. The Oxford English Corpus shows that in British English and many other varieties **learnt** is relatively common both as the past participle and the past tense: *I've really* learnt *a lot from TV, painters* learnt *their craft the hard way*. In North American English, however, these uses are rather uncommon. Using the form ending in **-ed** is therefore always a safe choice.

learning difficulties

The phrase **learning difficulties** covers a range of conditions, including Down's syndrome as well as cognitive or neurological conditions such as dyslexia. In emphasizing the difficulty experienced rather than any perceived 'deficiency' it is less discriminatory and more positive than older terms such as **mentally handicapped**. It is the phrase you should use to avoid the risk of causing offence and is the standard term in Britain in official contexts. **Learning disability** is the equivalent in North America, but in Britain that tends to refer specifically to conditions in which IQ is impaired.

lend

Lend is not a noun in standard English, where **loan** is the correct word to use. Though used informally in a number of dialects and varieties, as in *can I have a lend of your pen?*, it should be avoided in writing.

-less

When you are adding the ending **-less** to a word that already ends in a letter **-l** there is a simple rule to follow. If the first word ends in a *single* letter **-l** you do not need a hyphen, as in *soulless newbuild housing estates*; if it ends in **-ll** , you need a hyphen: *a small, wall-less town*. See also HYPHENATION.

less

In standard English, **less** should only be used with uncountable things (*less money*, *less time*). With countable things it is incorrect to use **less**; strictly speaking, correct use is *fewer people* and *fewer words*. For more information, see FEW.

lest

Lest remains one of the very few words in English with which (in good style) the subjunctive is used, as in *she was worrying lest he be attacked* (not *lest he was*. . .) or *she is using headphones lest she disturb anyone* (not . . . *lest she disturbs anyone*). It is also used with a conditional, as in *she is using headphones lest she should disturb anyone*, but in the Oxford English Corpus the subjunctive is ten times more common. See also SUBJUNCTIVE.

libel

Libel refers to a written untrue statement that is damaging to someone's reputation, while **slander** refers to the spoken expression of similar sentiments. Though the two are often used interchangeably it is useful to preserve the distinction in writing.

licence, license

It is easy to get confused about when to write **licence** and when **license**. Which spelling you choose depends on whether you are using the word as a noun or a verb, and whether you are following British usage or not. Spell the word with **c** in British

English when using it as a noun, as in *driving licence*, *off-licence*, *poetic licence*. When using it as verb, you should spell it with an **s**, as in *licensed premises*. Other varieties of English often follow this rule, except United States English, where the **-s-** is much more common in both the noun and the verb.

lie

Some forms of the verb **lie** are often confused with forms of the verb **lay**. See LAY.

life assurance, life insurance

There is a technical distinction between **life assurance** and **life insurance**: see ASSURANCE.

light

This is one of a small group of verbs which have alternative forms for the past tense and past participle. Both **lighted** and **lit** can be used in all varieties of English, but **lit** is much more common for the two forms mentioned. When you want to use the past participle before a noun, however, the two forms work differently. **Lighted** tends to be used when the verb is not modified in any way, as in *lighted windows*; *a lighted match*. When you modify the verb with an adverb, **lit** is much the more common form: *a brightly lit office*; *pleasantly lit corridors*.

lightning

The form **lightning** developed as a contracted form of *lightening* (the old spelling *light'ning* shows this process), but the two forms are now distinct words. In the meaning of *thunder and lightning* and *lightning speed*, the spelling is always **lightning**, When it means 'making or becoming lighter' the spelling is always **lightening**.

-like

When writing words ending in **-like** which are well established, such as *childlike*, *businesslike*, *dreamlike*, and *ladylike*, it is correct not to use a hyphen, even though you may come across such words written with one. In contrast, where the combination is a one-off or not fully established, you should insert a hyphen: *flu-like*, *Zen-like*, *needle-like*. For hyphen use with other adjectives, see HYPHENATION.

like

1 In the sentence *he's behaving like he owns the place*, **like** is a conjunction meaning 'as if', and it is best to avoid using it in written British English. Although **like** has been used as a conjunction in this way since the 15th century by many respected writers, it is still considered unacceptable in formal British English, where you should use **as if** instead.

2 Another use of **like** as a conjunction which many people object to is: *like I said, it's not possible*. This use is quite common in speech, but is likely to be considered incorrect in writing, where it is better to write *as I said, ...*

lit

For the use of **lighted** and **lit**, see LIGHT.

literally

In one of its meanings, **literally** is used to show that a metaphor or idiom is to be interpreted in its real, physical meaning, as in *literally too tired to move*. This use can lead to nonsense, as in *we were literally killing ourselves laughing*, so you should only use it in this way when you are sure that your audience will not take *you* literally.

loath, loathe

Loath and **loathe** are often confused in writing. **Loath** is an adjective meaning 'reluctant or unwilling', as in *I was loath to leave*, whereas **loathe** is a verb meaning 'feel intense dislike or disgust for', as in *she loathed him on sight*. **Loath** is occasionally written **loth**, which is also correct, even though it appears in fewer than five per cent of examples in the Oxford English Corpus. **Loath** and **loth** are pronounced the same, rhyming with *oath*.

locate

Locate is an 18th-century Americanism that still has a transatlantic flavour for some people, especially in its intransitive use (that is, without an object) as in *numerous industries have located in this area*. In both British and American English, **to be located** is a synonym for 'to be situated'—*the supermarket is located near a park*—but may cause disquiet among British purists.

lot

1 **A lot of** and **lots** of are very common in speech and writing, but they still have a somewhat informal feel and are generally not considered acceptable for formal English, where you should use alternatives such as *many* or *a large number of* instead.

2 If you do use **a lot** in writing, it is incorrect to write it as one word, although you may come across this spelling. For other words often written as one when they should be separated see TWO WORDS OR ONE.

luxurious, luxuriant

Luxurious and **luxuriant** are often confused, especially in marketing and promotional material. **Luxurious** means 'very comfortable, elegant, and involving great expense', as in *a luxurious hotel*, whereas **luxuriant** means 'lush', referring to vegetation, as in *acres of luxuriant gardens*. To speak of *luxuriant comfort* or *luxuriant four-poster beds*, for instance, would be considered incorrect by many people.

machinations

The **-ch-** in this word can be pronounced either as a **k** or as in *machine*, and both are acceptable.

machismo, macho

The **-ch-** in **machismo** can be pronounced either as a **k** or as in *church*, and both are acceptable, though the second is closer to the original Spanish. In **macho**, the **-ch-** is always pronounced as in *church*.

majority

Strictly speaking, **majority** should be used with countable nouns to mean 'the greater number', as in *the majority of cases*. Using it with uncountable nouns to mean 'the greatest part', as in *I spent the majority of the day reading*, is not considered good written English by purists, although it is common in informal contexts. It is still a cliché, and **the majority** is best replaced by **most**.

man, -man

There are two uses of **man** which many people may find objectionable nowadays. The first is when it refers to all human beings, as in *that's one small step for a man, one giant leap for mankind*, and the second is the use of **-man** in words denoting roles and activities, such as *fireman*.

Traditionally the word **man** was used to refer not only to adult males but also to human beings in general, regardless of sex. In Old English the principal meaning of *man* was 'a human being', and the words *wer* and *wif* were used to refer specifically to 'a male person' and 'a female person' respectively. Subsequently, **man** replaced *wer* as the normal term for 'a male person', but at the same time the older meaning of 'a human being' remained in use. Nowadays, this generic use of **man** will generally be regarded as sexist—or at best rather old-fashioned.

Similarly, since women are just as likely as men to be involved in all professions and activities, words for occupations and roles ending in -man, such as *fireman*, *layman*, and *chairman*, are increasingly being replaced by gender-neutral words: *firefighter*, *layperson*, and *chair* or *chairperson*.

In order to avoid being considered either an unreconstructed sexist or incorrigibly last-century it is therefore advisable to use alternatives to the more traditional words when the gender of the person concerned is not relevant. If the person referred to is a man, however, it is in general perfectly acceptable to use the word ending in *-man*: *he was a keen sportsman*. ▶

Below is a list giving suitable alternatives—some more established than others—for some of the most commonly used terms.

Generalizing

OLDER USAGE	NEWER USAGE
man	human beings, the human race
manhour	hour, person-hour
mankind	humankind, the human race, humanity
the man in the street	the person in the street, the average person, ordinary people, laypeople, people in the street

In one or two cases, such as *manpower* and *to man*, there are many alternatives, depending on the exact context, such as *staff*, *employees*, *people*, etc. and *to staff*, *to operate*, etc., respectively.

Professions

OLDER USAGE	NEWER USAGE	PLURAL
barman	bartender	bartenders, bar staff
businessman	businessperson	businesspeople
*chairman	chair, chairperson	chairpersons
clergyman	vicar, priest	the clergy
fellow		
countryman	compatriot	compatriots
fireman	firefighter	firefighters
freshman	fresher	freshers
layman	layperson	laypeople, the laity
policeman	police officer	police officers
salesman	salesperson	sales staff
spokesman	spokesperson	spokespeople
sportsman	sportsperson	sportspeople, sportsmen and sportswomen

*For referring to the head of a company, *chairman* is still the correct word.

manageress

See -ESS.

manic depression

Though terms that many people are familiar with, **manic depression** and **manic depressive** are sometimes felt to be negative by people experiencing the condition and those working with them. A less loaded term which is being increasingly used in medical and psychiatric circles is **bipolar disorder**, or **bipolar affective disorder**. People with the condition can be referred to simply as **bipolar**, or as **having bipolar disorder**.

man in the street

For a gender-neutral alternative, see MAN.

mankind

On the use of **mankind** versus that of **humankind** or **the human race**, see MAN.

masterful

Many people strive to maintain a distinction between **masterful** and **masterly**, using **masterful** to mean 'powerful and able to control others'—*a masterful tone of voice*—and **masterly** to mean 'with the skill of a master'—*a masterly performance*. In practice, the two words overlap considerably in this second meaning, and in the Oxford English Corpus most uses of **masterful** mean 'with the skill of a master'. But, if you are writing for a well-educated audience, maintaining the distinction will stand you in good stead.

maximum

Maximum is one of those Latin-derived words which have two plurals: the Latinate **maxima** and the English **maximums**. For guidance on when to use which, see the entry on LATIN PLURALS.

may

1 **May** and **might** are two ways of expressing that the truth of an event is unknown at the time of speaking or writing. Traditionalists insist that you should distinguish between **may** (present tense) and **might** (past tense): *I may have some dessert if I'm still hungry*; *she might have known her killer*. However, this distinction is rarely observed today, especially in informal usage, and **may** and **might** are generally acceptable in either case: *she may have visited yesterday*; *I might go and have a cup of tea*.

2 Whether you use **may have** or **might have**, though, is a different matter. If at the time of speaking or writing the truth is still not known, then either is acceptable: *by the time you read this, registration may have been received*; *I think that might have offended some people*.

3 However, if the event referred to did not in fact occur, it is best to use **might have**: *the draw against Arsenal might have been a turning point, but it didn't turn out like that*. **May have** is wrong in this example: *if they had been left the alternative verdict to consider, they may have focused their minds on it*.

4 On the difference in use between **may** and **can**, see CAN.

me

There are four cases where the choice between **me** and **I** can be problematic.

1 **I** should be used as the subject of the sentence, together with other people: *Trisha and I went out for a few months*; *he and I don't get on*. Though phrases such as *Trisha and me . . .*, *him and me . . .* are quite often used in speaking, they are grammatically wrong, and should be avoided.

2 **Me** should be used instead of **I** after a preposition, or as the object of a verb: *this letter is for you and me, they gave Jane and me a fantastic send-off*. Problems arise because people often think that it is correct to use **I** whenever other people are involved, as in the examples above. But this rule only applies to the subject of the sentence.

When you are referring to other people and yourself as the object of a verb or after a preposition, you need to replace **I** with **me**. So, it is not correct to write *a couple of guys flew from Germany to meet Tom and I at a convention*: it should be *Tom and me*. If you are in any doubt, try removing the other names from the sentence you are writing and it should then be clear whether **I** or **me** is appropriate. In the example just given you would not say: *a couple of guys flew from Germany to meet I at a convention*. Similarly, a concern to be correct often leads people to say *between you and I*, whereas *between you and me* is grammatically correct.

3 For advice on whether you should say *you have more than me* or *you have more than I*, see PERSONAL PRONOUN.

4 There is also some confusion over whether it is correct to say, for instance, *it was me that decided* or *it was I that decided*. The second is markedly more formal: it would, for instance, be very pompous indeed when announcing yourself to say *it is I* rather than *it's me*.

media

The word **media** comes from the Latin plural of **medium**. The traditional view is that it should therefore be treated as a plural noun in all its meanings in English and be used with a plural rather than a singular verb: *the media have not followed the reports* (rather than 'has'). In practice, in the meaning of 'television, radio, and the press collectively', it behaves as a collective noun (like *staff* or *clergy*, for example). This means that it is now acceptable in standard English to use it with either a singular or a plural verb, and few people are likely to object to its use with the first. See also COLLECTIVE NOUN.

memento

A **memento** of an occasion is something to remember it by. It comes from Latin, and means literally 'remember'. Although the variant spelling **momento** exists, many people will think you wrong if you use it. Think of all the letters **e** in **remember**, and it may help you to remember to put them in **memento** as well.

mental

Yesterday's euphemisms sometimes become today's insults, and **mental** is a case in point. Its use in compounds such as *mental hospital* and *mental patient* is first recorded at the end of the 19th century and became the normal accepted term in the first half of the 20th century. Now, however, it is regarded as certainly old-fashioned, if not offensive. The most usual acceptable alternative is *psychiatric*, which has already generally replaced it in official use. The particular terms **mental handicap** and **mentally handicapped**, though widely used a few decades ago, have fallen out of favour in recent years and have been largely replaced in official contexts by less demeaning terms such as **learning difficulties**.

merchandise

Merchandise and words derived from it, such as *merchandising*, are always correctly spelled with an s, not a z.

meter, metre

Meter is the normal spelling in both British and American English for the measuring or recording instrument, such as a *gas meter*. It is also the American English spelling for the unit of length and for 'rhythm in poetry', which in British English are both spelled **metre**.

might

On the distinction between **might** and **may**, see MAY.

militate

The verbs **militate** and **mitigate** are often confused. See MITIGATE.

millennium

The correct spelling is **millennium** with **-ll-** and **-nn-**. It may help you if you remember that the first part of the word means 'a thousand' in Latin, as in *millipede*, and is ultimately the basis for the word *million*. The second part is closely related to the word *annual*.

minimum

For information on which plural form to use, see LATIN PLURALS.

minuscule

The standard spelling is **minuscule** with a **u** in the second syllable rather than **miniscule**, with an **i**. The second form is a very common one, and appears in almost half the citations for the term in the Oxford English Corpus. It has been in use since the late 19th century, and arose by analogy with other words beginning with *mini-*, where the meaning is similarly 'very small'. It is now so widely used that it can be considered as an acceptable variant, although it should be avoided in formal contexts.

minutiae

Since **minutiae** is a word more often seen than heard, it can be hard to remember exactly how to pronounce it. The recommended pronunciation is /my-**nyoo**-shee/.

mischievous

Mischievous is a three-syllable word, pronounced /**miss**-chi-vuhs/. It should not be pronounced /miss-**chee**-vi-uhs/ with four syllables, as though it were spelled 'mischievious' (with an extra **i**), which is also wrong.

misspell

There are two possible forms for the past tense and past participle of this verb, **misspelled** and **misspelt**. Both are correct, although **misspelled** is much more common, while **misspelt** is rarely used at all outside British English.

mitigate

The verbs **mitigate** and **militate** do not mean the same thing, but their similarity leads to them often being confused. **Mitigate** means 'to make less severe', as in *drainage schemes have helped to mitigate this problem*. **Militate** is nearly always used in constructions with *against* to mean 'be a powerful factor in preventing', as in *these disagreements will militate against the two communities coming together*.

mongol, mongolism

The term **mongol** was adopted in the 19th century to refer to a person with **Down's syndrome** (and **mongolism** for the condition itself), owing to the supposed similarity of some of the physical symptoms of the disorder with the normal facial characteristics of East Asian people. In modern English these terms are offensive and have been replaced in scientific as well as in most general contexts by **Down's syndrome** (first recorded in the early 1960s), and related expressions such as *a person with Down's syndrome*, *a Down's baby*, etc.

Mongoloid

The terms **Mongoloid**, **Negroid**, **Caucasoid**, and **Australoid** were introduced by 19th-century anthropologists attempting to classify human racial types, but today they are recognized as having very limited validity as scientific categories. Although occasionally used when making broad generalizations about the world's populations, in most modern contexts they are potentially offensive, especially when used of individuals. The names of specific peoples, nationalities, or regions of the world should be used instead wherever possible.

moot

It is quite common to come across a debatable point being described as *'a mute point'*. This is a logical but mistaken adaptation of the old-established phrase **a moot point** and is generally not considered good style.

mouse

Unless we are very young children, we all know that we use **mice** to refer to more than one of these lovable rodents. But when we want to refer to more than one computer **mouse**, is it correct to say **mice** or **mouses**? You may sometimes hear **mouses**, but people seem to prefer the standard **mice**.

Muslim

Muslim is the preferred spelling for 'a follower of Islam' and 'relating to Islam', although the form **Moslem** is also used. The terms **Muhammadan** and **Mohammedan** are archaic and are likely to sound deliberately offensive.

mute

1 To describe a person without the power of speech as **mute**, especially as in **deaf mute**, is today regarded as outdated, and it is highly likely to cause offence. However, there is no direct, acceptable alternative, but *profoundly deaf* is used to imply that someone has not developed any spoken language skills. Compare DUMB.

2 For the phrase 'a mute point', see MOOT.

myself

There are two ways of using **myself** which nobody will object to, and two which some people will criticize. The innocuous uses are:

1 to show that the recipient of the action is the same as the speaker: *I hurt myself quite badly*.

2 to emphasize the word **I**: *I myself have no objection; I did it myself*.

The uses to which some people object are:

1 when **myself** is the subject of a verb: *the wife and myself had a wonderful time*.

2 when **myself** is the object of a verb: *they hauled Barry and myself in for questioning*.

Both these uses are perfectly acceptable in conversation. In more formal writing they should be avoided. In the case of 1 above, use **I**; and in the case of 2, use **me**. See also ME, YOURSELF.

Nama

The **Nama** people are one of the **Khoikhoi** peoples of South Africa and SW Namibia. They have in the past been called **Hottentot** (actually a somewhat broader term), but that is now obsolete and **Nama** is the standard accepted term. See HOTTENTOT.

native

In contexts such as *a native of Boston* the use of the noun **native** is quite acceptable. But when used as a noun without qualification, as in *this dance is a favourite with the natives*, it is more problematic. In modern use it can refer humorously to the local inhabitants of a particular place: *New York in the summer was too hot even for the natives*. However, it is likely to sound offensive if used to refer to any area of the world that has been under colonial rule, in which it was the standard term for indigenous people as opposed to their foreign masters.

Native American

Native American is now the current accepted term in most contexts, particularly in the US, for a member of any of the indigenous peoples of the United States, but see also AMERICAN INDIAN.

need

n

1 In modern English you can use the verb **need** followed by another verb in two different ways when asking a question or making a negative statement. One way is with *do* as in *I don't need to go just yet* and *do you really need to go?* The second way is without *do*, as in *I needn't go just yet* and *need you really go?* The two constructions are equally correct, but the construction using *do* is more common. In questions, the form without *do* is used especially in rhetorical questions: *need I say any more?*, *need I elaborate?*

When making a negative statement using **need** without *do*, the thing to remember is not to add on a letter s in the third person: *he need not worry*.

2 The two constructions in *that shirt needs washing* (verb + present participle) and *that shirt needs to be washed* (verb + infinitive and past participle) have more or less the same meaning. Both are acceptable in standard English, but a third construction, *that shirt needs washed* (verb + bare past

participle), is restricted to certain dialects of Scotland and North America and is not considered acceptable in standard English.

3 The phrase **if need be** has a long historical pedigree and is still widely used today. Traditionalists are likely to object to the form with the plural: *if needs be*.

Negro

The word **Negro** was adopted from Spanish and Portuguese and is first recorded in the mid 16th century. It remained the standard term from the 17th to the 19th century and was even used by prominent black American campaigners such as W. E. B. DuBois and Booker T. Washington in the early 20th century. Since the Black Power movement of the 1960s, however, when the term **black** was promoted as an expression of racial pride, **Negro** (together with related words such as **Negress**) has dropped out of use and is now likely to seem offensive in both British and US English.

Negroid

The term **Negroid** belongs to a set of terms introduced by 19th-century anthropologists attempting to categorize human races. Such terms are associated with outdated notions of racial types, and so are now potentially offensive and best avoided. See MONGOLOID.

neither

1 The use of **neither** with another negative, as in *I don't like him neither* or *he's not much good at reading neither* is recorded from the 16th century onwards, but is not good English. This is because it is an example of a **double negative**, which, though standard in some other languages such as French and Spanish and found in many dialects of English, is not acceptable in standard English. In the sentences above, **either** should be used instead. For more information, see DOUBLE NEGATIVE.

2 When **neither** is followed by **nor**, it is important in good English style that the two halves of the structure mirror each other: *she saw herself as neither wife nor mother* rather than *she*

neither saw herself as wife nor mother. *For more details, see* EITHER.

3 It is equally correct to pronounce **neither** as /**nI**-*th*uh/ or /**nee**-*th*uh/.

nerve-racking, nerve-wracking

Both spellings are used in British and American English and are correct, although in British English there are more examples of the spelling with a **w**.

neuron

In scientific material the standard spelling is **neuron**. The spelling **neurone** is found only in non-technical contexts.

nevertheless

It is quite common to find **nevertheless** spelled 'never the less'. Although this is how it was written many centuries ago, the standard modern spelling is as one word. For more information, see TWO WORDS OR ONE.

niggardly

Niggardly has no historical connection whatsoever with *nigger*, but because it sounds similar, and probably because it has a negative meaning—'ungenerous with money, time, etc.' or 'mean'—it is wise to avoid it outside literary contexts. Politicians, both in the US and the UK, have been severely embarrassed by having used it.

nigger

The word **nigger** was first used (as an adjective, in fact) to denote a black person in the 17th century, and it has long had derogatory overtones. However, it has not been seen as generally offensive for as long: Bertie Wooster, in a P. G. Wodehouse novel of 1934, refers to 'a troupe of nigger minstrels', and Guy Gibson, the leader of the 'Dambusters' in the Second World War, called his black dog Nigger, and that name was used in the film made in 1954. The scenes in which it is referred to are edited out of some showings nowadays, as the word is now possibly the single most offensive word in English. It is true that it is sometimes used by black people themselves to refer to other black people, but in any other context it is unacceptable.

noisome

Noisome is a relatively uncommon word meaning 'harmful, noxious' and has nothing to do with the word **noise**. It comes from a Middle English word **nay**, related to **annoy**. Purists will object to its being used to mean 'noisy'.

non-

For a comparison of the prefixes **non-** and **un-**, see UN-.

non-defining relative clauses

See RELATIVE CLAUSES.

none

Some language purists maintain that **none** can only take a singular verb, never a plural one: *none of them* is *coming tonight* rather than *none of them* are *coming tonight*. There is little historical or grammatical justification for this view. **None** comes from Old English *nan* meaning 'not one' and has been used for around a thousand years with both a singular and a plural verb, depending on the context and the emphasis needed. see also AGREEMENT.

nonetheless

It is quite common to find **nonetheless** spelled 'none the less'. Although this is how it was written many centuries ago, the standard modern spelling is as one word. For more information see TWO WORDS OR ONE.

non-flammable, non-inflammable

The adjectives **non-flammable** and **non-inflammable** mean the same; see FLAMMABLE.

nonplussed

In standard use **nonplussed** means 'surprised and confused', as in *she was nonplussed at his eagerness to help out*. In North American English a new use has developed in recent years, meaning 'unperturbed'—more or less the opposite of its traditional meaning—as in *he was clearly trying to appear nonplussed*. Although the use is common it is not yet considered standard. Similarly, many people would not consider spelling this word with a hyphen, **non-plussed**, to be good style.

non-restrictive relative clauses

See RELATIVE CLAUSES.

non-white

Many people object to the term **non-white** on the grounds that it assumes that the norm is white. It is difficult to find a widely acceptable and accurate alternative: *person of colour* is rather stilted, and *ethnic* too euphemistic for many, but 'black or Asian' is an effective substitute in Britain (see ASIAN). If you are talking about a person or number of people from only one racial group, it is simpler to refer to that group.

normalcy

Normalcy has been criticized as an uneducated alternative to **normality**. The Oxford English Corpus shows that in the United States and Canada it is as common as **normality**, and it is the preferred form in Indian English. Elsewhere it is less common and has a distinctly American flavour, which purists, especially in Britain, are likely to object to.

noun

A **noun** is a word that names a person, animal, or thing. Common nouns name persons, animals, or things of which there is not just one example (*bridge, girl, sugar, unhappiness*), whereas proper nouns name specific people, places, events, institutions, magazines, books, plays, and so forth, and are written with initial capital letters (*Billy, Asia, Easter, Hamlet*). Concrete nouns refer to physical things and living beings (*bread, woman*), and abstract nouns to concepts (*greed, unhelpfulness*). Some nouns are concrete and abstract in different meanings, e.g. *cheek* is concrete when it refers to a part of the face and abstract when it means 'impertinence'.

nouns, singular and plural

No language stays still, least of all English. Among the myriad changes which take place over the course of time, some words change 'number': some which were singular become plural, and vice versa. Our modern **pea** was formed from *pease*. Once the singular, based directly on the French, its **-s** sound at the end was interpreted as a plural, and so a new singular was created. **News**, on the other hand, was for many centuries plural as well as singular, so that Shelley could write *There are bad news from Palermo*.

With some loanwords (words 'borrowed' from other languages), there is uncertainty over which form is the singular, and which the plural. In the past many of these nouns came from Greek and Latin; when those two languages were widely studied, it was expected that people would be familiar enough with their grammar to know that, for instance, **criterion** was a singular form in Greek and its plural was **criteria**. Nowadays, however, most people have little or no knowledge of either language and many make perfectly reasonable assumptions about them which happen to be wrong historically. If someone does not know Latin, it is perfectly sensible for them to think that **addenda** is a singular, like *agenda*, and give it a plural **addendas**.

PLURALS USED AS SINGULAR	SINGULAR FORM IN ORIGINAL LANGUAGE
addenda	addendum
bacteria	bacterium
bijoux (as adjective)	bijou
cherubim	cherub

criteria	criterion
errata	erratum
panini	panino
phenomena	phenomenon
strata	stratum
tableaux	tableau

All of these plurals used as a singular would be regarded as mistakes, except **panini**, which is now established in English as the singular form, with **paninis** as an acceptable plural. Other such 're-pluralizations', made by adding an English plural ending, are not acceptable, e.g. *'cherubims'*, *'criterias'*, and *'stratas'*.

By contrast, a loanword whose singular form looks like an English plural, such as **biceps**, may well be altered to produce a 'proper-looking' singular. This has produced *'bicep'* meaning one biceps muscle, but it is considered incorrect. To compound the confusion, *biceps*, being singular, sometimes has an English plural ending added, just to make sure, as it were, producing *'bicepses'*. Neither *bicep* nor *bicepses* is recommended.

Some loanwords mislead people into using spurious foreign plurals: **addenda**, as mentioned above, is already a plural, but is sometimes mistakenly turned into *'addendae'* on the grounds that many Latin nouns ending in *-a* become *-ae*, e.g. *alga*, *algae*. This can also happen to **agenda**. *Octopus* is often mistakenly given the plural *'octopi'* because many Latin nouns ending in *-us* change to *-i*, but **octopus** is from Greek. **Ignoramus** comes from the name of a 17th-century fictional character and was never a noun in Latin, so the correct plural is *ignoramuses*, not *'ignorami'*. **Kudos** is an interesting case. It is traditionally used as an uncountable singular noun, like **fame**, with only a singular form: *he earned a lot of kudos for his resistance*. However, many people seem to be using it to mean an award, point, or congratulation for something well done. As a result, a singular *'kudo'* has been created, as well as the plurals *'kudoses'* and, almost inexplicably, *'kudi'*.

number

The construction **the number of** + plural noun should be used with a singular verb, as in *the number of people affected remains small*. This is because it is the noun **number** rather than the noun **people** which is taken to agree with the verb. In contrast, the similar construction **a number of** + plural noun is used with a plural verb: *a number of people remain to be contacted*. In this case the verb agrees with the noun **people**. This is because **a number of** works as if it were a single word, such as **some** or **several**.

numerals

The main question about numbers is whether to write them as figures or as words. The following are some basic guidelines.

In general, numerals are used in more factual or statistical contexts and words are used (especially with numbers under a hundred) in more descriptive material: compare *I have lived in the same house for twelve years* with *the survey covers a period of 12 years*.

It is usual to use words rather than figures at the beginning of sentences: *Sixty-four people came to the party*.

Words are used in idiomatic expressions such as *I must have told you a hundred times; thousands of people swarmed through the gates*.

Separate objects, animals, ships, persons, etc. are not units of measurement unless they are treated statistically: *the peasant had only four cows; a farm with 40 head of cattle*.

Whether written as figures or words, plurals of numbers are written without an apostrophe: *the 1970s, a man in his thirties, they come in twos*.

With numerals consisting of four or more figures, ▶

commas should be used to divide off the thousands, e.g. *3,096*, *10,731*.

When specifying ranges of numbers, use as few figures as possible, e.g. *31–4*; *1923–6*. But dates BC should be written in full: *432–431* BC (since *432–31* BC and *432–1* BC represent different ranges).

More detailed information will be found in *New Hart's Rules*, published in 2005 by Oxford University Press.

obtuse

Obtuse and **abstruse** are often confused. Someone who is **obtuse** is rather stupid, as in *she's about as obtuse as they come*. Something which is **abstruse** is rather obscure and difficult to understand. To use **obtuse** in the meaning of 'obscure, difficult', though often done, is not considered good style, and conservatives will consider it a rank mistake.

occurrence

The letter **u** in **occurrence** is normally pronounced like the **u** of **cut**. Some people pronounce it in the same way as in the verb (/uh-**ker**-uhns/), but this is wrong.

octopus

The standard plural of **octopus** in English is **octopuses**. The word comes from Greek, but the Greek plural **octopodes** is almost never used genuinely (i.e. outside writing about the plural of **octopus**). The plural form **octopi**, formed according to the rules of Latin plurals, is incorrect. See also LATIN PLURALS.

of

It is a mistake to use **of** instead of **have** in constructions such as *you should have asked* (not *you should* of *asked*). For more information, see HAVE.

off

The compound preposition **off of** is sometimes used interchangeably with the preposition **off** in a context such as *she picked it up off of the floor* compared with *she picked it up off the floor*. The use of **off of** is recorded from the 16th century, was used commonly by Shakespeare, for example, and is logically parallel to **out of**, but is not accepted in standard modern English. Today **off of** is restricted to dialect and informal contexts, particularly in the US.

offence, offense

The spelling **offence** with a letter **c** is standard in nearly all varieties of English, except in the US, where **offense** with an **s** is the norm. To use this second spelling in a non-US context is therefore likely to be considered incorrect.

offspring

The meaning of **offspring** covers both an individual child and several children, though the latter meaning is the more common. As a result, the word does not need the plural form '*offsprings*' with an **-s** which is sometimes encountered.

oftentimes

Though somewhat rare outside the US, and likely to sound archaic to a British ear, **oftentimes** is a perfectly acceptable and standard alternative to **often**, as in: *oftentimes the dialogue has an unnatural ring*.

on-board, on board

Should you write **on-board** or **on board**? It depends on the meaning. If you are talking about passengers on a ship or plane, you would say they are **on board**: *the plane crashed with twenty people on board*. You also write **on board** in non-literal phrases like *to take something on board* and *to bring someone on board*. You write **on-board** with a hyphen if you are talking about a piece of equipment or computer fitted into a car, boat, plane, or other vehicle: *on-board DVD players for the kids*.

one

1 **One** is used as a pronoun to mean 'anyone' or 'me and people in general', as in *one must try one's best*. In modern English it is generally only used in formal and written contexts, outside which it is likely to be regarded as pompous or over-formal.

In informal and spoken contexts the normal alternative is **you**, as in *you have to do what you can, don't you?*

2 When **one** means 'anyone', British and American English use different pronouns to refer back to it. In British English another **one** or **one's** always follows: *one should be especially careful if one already uses prescription anti-coagulants*. In American English this pattern is possible, but it is also common to use **he**, **she** (or **they**, to avoid gender problems), and **his**, **her**, and **their**: *I like to believe one can be honest and sincere and committed in what he's doing*.

3 When using phrases such as *one in ten people* or *one out of every six people interviewed*, you need to be careful with the following verb. It should be singular, not plural, when it refers back to **one**: *only one in ten men affected* ***is*** *seeking treatment*, not *one in ten businesses* ***are*** *owned by ethnic minorities*. See also AGREEMENT.

online

Is it correct to write **online** or **on line** to describe things you do over the Internet? The first thing to think about is how exactly you are using the word. Does it relate to a noun, as in *online shopping*, *online banking*, and *online dating*? Or does it relate to an adjective or verb: *now available online*; *you can register online*? In the first case, there is no choice: you should write **online** as one word. In the second case, you could in principle write it either way. However, people write it as one word much more often than as two, and Oxford Dictionaries Online show it in this form.

only

The traditional view is that the adverb **only** should be placed next to the word or words whose meaning it restricts: *I have seen him only once* rather than *I have only seen him once*. The argument for this, a topic which has occupied grammar experts for more than 200 years, is that if **only** is not placed correctly the emphasis may be wrong, and could even lead to ambiguity. But in normal, everyday English the impulse is to state **only** as early as possible in the sentence, generally just before the verb. The result is, in fact, hardly ever ambiguous. Few people would be confused by the sentence *I have only seen him once*, and the supposed 'logical' meaning often emerges only if there is further clarification, as in *I've only seen him once, but I've heard him many times.*

onto

The preposition **onto**, meaning 'to a position on the surface of', as in *they fell off their stools onto the rough stone floor*, has been widely written as one word (instead of **on to**) since the early 18th century. Some people, however, still do not wholly accept it as part of standard English (unlike **into**, for example). In US English, **onto** is more or less the standard form and this is likely to become the case in British English before long.

Because of the increasing tendency to write the two words as one, it is important to remember never to write **on to** as one word when it means 'onwards and towards', as in *let's go on to the next point*.

or

1 Where a verb follows a list separated by **or**, the traditional rule is that the verb should be singular, as long as the things in the list are individually singular, as in *a sandwich or other snack is included in the price* (rather than *a sandwich or other snack are included in the price*). The argument is that each of the elements agrees separately with the verb precisely because they are alternatives. The opposite rule applies when the elements are joined by **and**: here, the verb should be plural, *a sandwich and a cup of coffee are included in the price*. These traditional rules should be observed in good English writing style but are often disregarded in speech.

2 On the use of **either . . . or**, see EITHER.

oriental

The term **oriental** has an out-of-date feel when used to refer to people from the Far East. It tends to be associated with a rather offensive stereotype of the people and their customs as exotic and inscrutable. In US English, **Asian** is the standard accepted term in modern use; in British English, where **Asian** tends to denote specifically people from the Indian subcontinent, it is better to use precise terms such as **Chinese**, **Japanese**, and so forth.

ought

The verb **ought** is a *modal verb*, which means that it does not behave grammatically like ordinary verbs. In particular, the negative is formed with the word **not** alone and not with auxiliary verbs such as **do** or **have**. Therefore the standard construction for the negative is *he ought not to have gone*. The alternative forms *he didn't ought to have gone* and *he hadn't ought to have gone*, formed as though **ought** were an ordinary verb rather than a modal verb, are found in dialect from the 19th century but are not acceptable in standard modern English.

ours

There is no need for an apostrophe: the spelling should be **ours** not **our's**.

ourself

The standard reflexive form corresponding to **we** and **us** is **ourselves**, as in *we can only blame ourselves*. The singular form **ourself**, first recorded in the 15th century, is sometimes used in modern English, typically where 'we' refers to people in general. This use, though logical, is uncommon and not generally accepted in standard English. Compare THEMSELF.

out

The use of **out** as a preposition rather than the standard prepositional phrase **out of**, as in *he threw it out the window*, is common in informal contexts but is not widely accepted in standard British English.

output

The past tense and past participle of **output** as a verb can be either **output** or **outputted.** The first is more common and the second may strike a jarring note for more traditional speakers. See VERBS FORMED FROM NOUNS.

outside

There is no difference in meaning between **outside** and **outside of** as in *the books have been distributed outside Europe* and *the books have been distributed outside of Europe*. The use of

outside of is much commoner and better established in North American than in British English.

overly

The use of **overly** in place of the prefix **over-**, e.g. *overly confident* instead of *over-confident*, although not uncommon and well established in British usage, is still likely to be regarded as an Americanism by more conservative speakers and could well strike a jarring note.

oversimplistic

Many language purists would argue that **oversimplistic** is an unnecessary word, and that it says the same thing twice, since **simplistic** already means 'over-simple'. It is therefore best to avoid it in formal contexts.
See also SIMPLISTIC.

overused words

Some words and phrases are trotted out over and over again, unthinkingly and without proper regard to their context, so that any lustre they may have once had is soon worn away through overhandling. They can be loosely grouped into the twin categories of (a) clichés proper and (b) modish technical words and phrases in general use. In both cases it is worth asking yourself:

- what exactly the word or phrase adds to what you are trying to say
- whether it expresses what you really want to express
- whether removing it would detract from the meaning you want to communicate.

Clichés

The French word *cliché* means a stereotype printing block, which produces the same page over and over again. It was first used in this meaning in English, before acquiring ▶

its modern meaning in 1892. A cliché is a phrase that has become meaningless with overuse, or, as the *Oxford Dictionary of English* pithily defines it, 'a phrase or opinion that is overused and betrays a lack of original thought'. For instance, it is now almost meaningless to wish someone *Have a nice day* because the once sincere intention has become an empty formula.

Clichés range from once striking metaphors, such as *the tip of the iceberg*, to conversational formulas, such as *not to put too fine a point on it*, and stereotyped combinations of words, as in *to unveil plans*, *a robust defence*, *to open a dialogue with*, etc.

In everyday language it would probably be rather difficult to communicate without occasional recourse to what some critics would regard as clichés: *when all's said and done*, the aim in ordinary conversation is not originality but getting your message across. However, most authorities suggest that, when it comes to original writing, clichés should be used sparingly: 'Yesterday's daring metaphors are today's clichés,' as Arthur Koestler put it. Clichés are often the refuge of the journalist with a deadline and the politician in a tight corner. No doubt we all have our own list of most irritating overworked phrases, and what follows is just a short list of some typical ones:

at this moment/point in time
by and large
conspicuous by one's absence
constructive dialogue
draw a line under
explore every avenue
full and frank exchange of views
I hear what you're saying
in the 21st century
keep a low profile
last but not least

put your head above the parapet
take something on board
take your eye off the ball

Technical terms

Technical terms are terms which are used by people in a particular field of activity and have a very precise meaning. They often pass into mainstream use (*mainstream* itself being a case in point), and this is one of the standard ways in which English is enriched through metaphors. Classic examples are *to be in the limelight*, from the intense white light produced by heating lime which was used in Victorian theatres, and *the acid test*, from the test for gold using nitric acid. Problems occur when a technical term is used incorrectly or in a way which attempts to blind the reader with science. Some very visible examples are:

crescendo
exponentially
factor (as noun and verb)
interface (as noun and verb)
leading-edge
learning curve
order of magnitude
product
profile
think outside the box
zero-sum game

owing

For an explanation of the difference between **owing to** and **due to**, see DUE.

panini

See NOUNS, SINGULAR AND PLURAL.

participle

There are two kinds of participle in English: the present participle ending with **-ing**, as in *we are going*, and the past participle, generally ending with **-d** or **-ed** for many verbs and with other letters in other verbs, as in *have you decided?*; *new houses are being built*; *it's not broken*. Participles are often used in writing to introduce subordinate clauses that relate to other words in a sentence, e.g. *her mother, **opening** the door quietly, came into the room*, where it is *her mother* who is opening the door. Other examples are: ***hearing** a noise I went out to look*; ***having been born** in Rochdale, he spent most of his life in the area*.

1 Participles at the beginning of a sentence, as in the last two examples, are perfectly acceptable grammatically, but when they are overused they can produce a poor style. They are especially poor style when the clause they introduce has only a weak logical link with the main clause: ***being** blind from birth, she became a teacher and travelled widely*. It is therefore advisable in your writing to make sure that any participles you use at the beginning of a sentence are strongly linked to what follows them.

2 A worse stylistic error occurs with so-called 'dangling participles'. Participles 'dangle' when the action they describe is not being performed by the subject of the sentence. Interpreted very literally, the sentence *recently converted into apartments, I passed by the house where I grew up* implies that the person writing has recently been converted into apartments. Here is another example: *driving near home recently, a thick pall of smoke turned out to be a bungalow well alight*. Although we know exactly what these two examples mean, unattached participles can ▶

P

distract and sometimes genuinely mislead the reader and are best avoided.

3 A small group of participles, which include *allowing for, assuming, considering, excepting, given, including, provided, seeing (as/that)*, and *speaking (of)* have become prepositions or conjunctions in their own right, and their use when unrelated to the subject of the sentence is now standard and perfectly acceptable, as in *speaking of money, how much did this all cost?*

peak, peek

The word meaning 'to look quickly or furtively' and 'a quick or furtive look' is written **peek**, not **peak**: *the sun peeks out only intermittently; a sneak peek at what's in store.*

pence

Both **pence** and **pennies** have existed as the plural of **penny** since at least the 16th century. Nowadays, the two forms tend to be used for different purposes: **pence** refers to sums of money (*five pounds and sixty-nine pence*) while **pennies** refers to the coins themselves (*I put pennies in my piggy bank*). In recent years, **pence** rather than **penny** has often sometimes been used in the singular to refer to amounts of one penny: *the Chancellor will put one pence on income tax*. The coin itself is stamped **penny**, not **pence**, and this singular use of **pence** is not standard English.

peninsula

The spelling of the noun as **peninsular** instead of **peninsula** is a common mistake; around 20 per cent of examples in the Oxford English Corpus are for the incorrect spelling. The spelling **peninsula** should be used when a noun is intended (*the end of the Cape Peninsula*), whereas **peninsular** is the spelling of the adjective (*the peninsular part of Malaysia*).

penny

On the different uses of the plural forms **pence** and **pennies**, see PENCE.

perceive

The core meaning of **perceive** is 'to become aware of or notice something', especially through your senses: *she perceived that all was not well; I perceived a change in his behaviour.* Used with that meaning it is rather formal in tone. But it is far more widely used with a different meaning, as a high-falutin' way of saying **see, consider**, or **regard**: *some geographers perceive hydrology to be a separate field*. When used that way it is arguably somewhat pretentious, not to mention laden with psychological baggage. The alternatives mentioned above work as well, or better, in most cases.

perfect

The traditional pronunciation of **perfect** as an adjective is with an **i** sound in the second syllable: /**pur**-fikt/, as Lou Reed famously sang in his anthemic *Perfect Day*. There is now a widespread tendency to pronounce the second syllable as in **bed**, perhaps under the influence of the 'speak as you spell' school of thought. Only time will tell if the older pronunciation eventually becomes extinct, but currently the chances of its survival are not looking good.

perpetrate, perpetuate

The words **perpetrate** and **perpetuate** are sometimes confused. **Perpetrate** means 'to commit a harmful, illegal, or immoral action', as in *a crime has been perpetrated against a sovereign state*, whereas **perpetuate** means 'to make something continue indefinitely', as in *a monument to perpetuate the memory of those killed in the war*.

-person

The use of **-person**, instead of *-man*, as a gender-neutral suffix denoting occupations, began in the 1970s with *chairperson* (see CHAIRMAN). Although coining these words was in principle a laudable attempt to reduce sexism enshrined in the language, their use in practice, as demonstrated by the Oxford English Corpus, has spread rather more slowly than might have been expected. One reason for this may be that people are reluctant to adopt forms that, while more politically correct, are linguistically more awkward or cumbersome. In some cases they sound almost fundamentalist or are deliberately contrived or ironic, as in *fisherperson*, *clergyperson*, *henchperson*, or *snowperson*. One solution has been to use a different word, such as *firefighter* instead of *fireman* or *fireperson*, and *police officer* instead of *policeman* or *policewoman*. People are also finding other ways of expressing the professions and roles concerned: for instance, instead of referring to someone as a *barman* or *barperson* (let alone *barmaid*), one hears *a member of the bar staff* or that someone *works behind the bar*.

It is also interesting that the most widely used forms according to the Corpus, namely *spokesperson* and *chairperson*, come from the area of public life and are often used in official and news documents. Even so, *spokesperson* in the Corpus is about a quarter as frequent as *spokesman*, and slightly less frequent than *spokeswoman*, but this could be because these terms are commonly used of a particular person, when there is felt to be less need to be gender-neutral.

The list below gives the 'top ten' from the Corpus, starting with the most frequent, and their year of coinage, where known. As can be seen, most of them are 1970s creations.

spokesperson 1972
chairperson 1971

p

salesperson	1971
layperson	1972
sportsperson	
businessperson	
foreperson	1973
craftsperson	1976
congressperson	1972
tradesperson	1886

The substitution of *person* for *man* in other ways, e.g. in *personhandle*, *personpower*, and *gingerbread person*, still shows little sign of being taken seriously.

personally

Personally has two unobjectionable uses, illustrated by:

- *the decision was made by the president personally* ('by the president and no one else'), and
- *he took the criticism personally* ('in a personal manner').

Some people, however, object to **personally** being used to mean 'for myself, for my part', as in *personally, I don't approve of such behaviour*. Although using the word in this way is a very useful way of emphasizing your own view, it is best restricted to informal contexts. In many cases it can be simply omitted, or replaced by the more formal *for my part*. Less acceptable is using the word in this meaning when the 'person' is not referred to at all, as in *personally, that would be nice*.

personal pronoun

1 The correct use of personal pronouns is one of the trickier areas of English usage. **I**, **we**, **they**, **he**, and **she** are known technically as **subjective** personal pronouns because they are used as the subject of a sentence, often coming before the verb (*she lives in Paris*; *we are leaving*). **Me**, ▶

us, **them**, **him**, and **her**, on the other hand, are called **objective** personal pronouns because they are used as the object of a verb, or following a preposition (*John hates me*; *his father left him*; *I did it for her*).

The distinction made above explains why it is incorrect to say either *John and me went to the shops* or *John and her went to the shops*: the personal pronoun is in subject position, so it must be **I** not **me**, and **she** not **her**. Using the pronoun alone makes the incorrect use obvious: *me went to the shops* is clearly not acceptable.

This analysis also explains why it is incorrect to say *he came with you and I*: the personal pronoun follows the preposition **with** and is therefore objective, so it must be **me** not **I**. Again, a simple test for correctness is to use the pronoun alone: *he came with I* is clearly not acceptable. (See also BETWEEN.)

2 Where a personal pronoun is used alone without a verb or a preposition, however, the traditional analysis starts to break down. Traditionalists sometimes argue, for example, that *she's younger than me* and *I've not been here as long as her* are incorrect and should be *she's younger than I* and *I've not been here as long as she*. Their argument is based on the assumption that **than** and **as** are conjunctions and so the personal pronoun is still subjective even though there is no verb; they argue that there is an implied verb, i.e. *she's younger than I am*. Yet the supposed 'correct' form does not sound natural at all to most speakers of English and is almost never used in speech.

It might be more accurate to say that in modern English those personal pronouns listed above as being **objective** are used 'neutrally'—i.e. they are used in all cases where the pronoun is not explicitly **subjective**. From this it follows that it is standard and perfectly acceptable English to use any of the following: *who is it? it's me!*; *she's taller than him*; *I didn't do as well as her*. Those who would consider these last examples as wrong are attempting to dictate the grammar of English, using the grammar of Latin as their yardstick.

perspective

Perspective is well established in the meaning of 'point of view', as in: *from our perspective this is a sensible proposal*. Nowadays it is increasingly common to encounter phrases where **perspective** is replaced by **prospective**: *from our prospective this is a sensible proposal*. Though there are historical precedents for **prospective** being used in this way, it is best to avoid doing so, as many people, especially British speakers, will regard such a use as a mistake.

peruse

Peruse is a rather formal word with the very specific meaning 'to read something in a very thorough and careful way': *he has spent countless hours in libraries perusing art history books*. Many people mistakenly think it means 'to read something through quickly', as in *documents will be perused rather than analysed thoroughly*. To use it in this way is not only wrong, but may also confuse your listener or reader.

phenomenon

The word **phenomenon** comes from Greek, and its plural form is **phenomena**, as in *these phenomena are not fully understood*. You will quite often come across **phenomena** used as a singular form, as in *this is a strange phenomena*, but it is best to stick to the traditional singular and plural distinction. For similar examples, see NOUNS, SINGULAR AND PLURAL.

phosphorus, phosphorous

The correct spelling for the noun denoting the chemical element is **phosphorus**, while the correct spelling for the adjective meaning 'relating to or containing phosphorus' is **phosphorous**. Over 90 per cent of the examples of **phosphorous** in the Oxford English Corpus should have been spelled **phosphorus**. Note that some uses which sound adjectival, such as *a phosphorus bomb* and *the deadline for reducing phosphorus levels*, in fact use the noun as a modifier and are therefore spelled **-rus**. True adjectives are found in expressions such as *phosphorous acid*.

pianist

People on both sides of the Atlantic commonly find that 'America and England are two countries separated by a common language', as George Bernard Shaw put it. That his witticism has more than a grain of truth is graphically illustrated by a word as seemingly straightforward as **pianist**. In Britain you put the stress very firmly on the letter **i**: /**pee**-uh-nist/. Stateside, you stress it in the same way as you would *piano*, with the stress very firmly on the letter **a**: /pee-**a**-nist/.

plead

In a law court a person can **plead guilty** or **plead not guilty**. The phrase **plead innocent** is not a technical legal term, though it is commonly found in general use.

plethora

A **plethora** is not simply an abundance of something, but rather an overabundance, as in: *the bill had to struggle through a plethora of committees and subcommittees.*
In sentences such as *a plethora of play spaces and equipment*, the looser meaning of 'abundance' is often not considered good style.

pore, pour

Pour and **pore** are often confused. If you want to describe 'studying or reading something intensely' with the phrase to **pore over**, the correct spelling is as shown, not **pour**.

practice, practise

It is easy to get confused about when to write **practice** and when **practise**. Which spelling you should choose depends on whether you're using the word as a noun or a verb, and whether you're following British usage or not. In British English spell the word with a **c** when using it as a noun, as in *practice makes perfect*. When using one of its verbal forms you should spell it with an **s**, as in *practising Christians*. In the US the word is always spelled with a **c**.

pre-

The prefix **pre-** is often joined to the word it qualifies without a hyphen, e.g. *prearrange*, *predetermine*, *preoccupy*. But when the word begins with **e-** or **i-**, or if it looks like another word, it is usual to insert a hyphen, e.g. *pre-eminent, pre-ignition, pre-position* (to distinguish it from *preposition*).

preferable, preferably

Both **preferable** and **preferably** are traditionally pronounced with the stress on the first syllable, in British and American English: /**pref**-ruh-buhl/, /**pref**-ruh-bli/.

preposition

A preposition is a word such as *after*, *in*, *to*, or *with*, which usually comes before a noun or pronoun and establishes the way it relates to what has gone before (*the man* ***on*** *the platform, they came* ***after*** *dinner*, and *what did you do it* ***for***?).

The superstition that a preposition should always precede the word it governs and should not end a sentence, as it does in the last example given above, seems to have developed from an observation by the 17th-century poet John Dryden. It is not based on a real appreciation of the structure of English, which regularly separates words that are grammatically related.

There are cases when it is either impossible or sounds stilted to organize the sentence in a way that avoids a preposition at the end, as demonstrated by Churchill's famous *This is the sort of English up with which I will not put*. By the same token, the pithy phrase *I want to meet the people worth talking to* becomes convoluted when reorganized as *I want to meet the people with whom it is worthwhile to talk*.

The following are cases where it is generally impossible to reorganize the sentence.

▶

First, in relative clauses and questions featuring phrasal verbs (verbs with linked adverbs or prepositions): *what did Marion think she was up to?*; *they must be convinced of the commitment they are taking on*; *budget cuts themselves are not damaging: the damage depends on where the cuts are coming from*.

Second, in passive constructions: *the dress had not even been paid for*; *we were well looked after*.

Last, in short sentences including an infinitive with *to*: *there are a couple of things I want to talk to you about*.

In conclusion, in more formal writing you might consider not leaving a preposition dangling at the end of the sentence when you are absolutely sure that putting it elsewhere will not result in the sentence becoming stilted or unnatural. Generally, however, finishing a sentence with a preposition is a natural part of the structure of English; those who object to it are perpetuating an antiquated shibboleth.

presently

Presently has two meanings. The older, meaning 'now', dates from the 15th century and is the dominant meaning in American English, as in *he is presently chair of the committee*. The second meaning is 'in a while, soon', and used to be the chief meaning in British English, as in *he will see you presently*. Nowadays the first meaning is just as common in British English as the second, and just as correct, despite the objections of some traditionalists.

principal, principle

The words **principal** and **principle** sound the same but mean different things. **Principle** is normally used as a noun meaning 'a fundamental truth or basis underlying a system of thought or belief', as in *this is one of the basic principles of democracy*. **Principal** is normally an adjective meaning 'main or most important', as in *one of the country's principal cities*. **Principal** can also be a noun when used to refer to the most important or senior person in an organization: *the deputy principal, a principal with the Royal Ballet*.

program, programme

The standard spelling of the noun and verb in British English is **programme**, except when referring to computer programs: *TV programme*; *programme of study*; *he programmes the film festival every year*; but *computer program*, *can you program in Perl?* In American English and most other varieties **program** is used for the noun and verb in all contexts. When used as a verb, the forms are **programming**, **programmes** or **programs**, according to context, and **programmed**. In the US the spellings with a single **m**, **programing** and **programed** are accepted, though not very common.

pronouns

A pronoun is a word such as *I*, *we*, *they*, *me*, *you*, *them*, etc., and other forms such as the possessive *hers*, *theirs*, and so forth and the reflexive *myself*, *themselves*, etc. They are used to refer to and take the place of a noun or noun phrase that has already been mentioned or is known, especially in order to avoid repetition, as in the sentence *when Jane saw her husband again, she wanted to hit him*.

When a pronoun refers back to a person or thing previously named, it is important that the gap is not so large that the reader or hearer might have difficulty relating the two, and that ambiguity is avoided when more than one person might be referred to. Here is an example (where the ambiguity is deliberate) from a play by Tom Stoppard:

SEPTIMUS: Geometry, Hobbes assures us in the *Leviathan*, is the only science God has been pleased to bestow on mankind.

LADY CROOM: And what does he mean by it?
SEPTIMUS: Mr Hobbes or God?

pronunciation

People often say the second syllable of **pronunciation** as -ouns- (pruh-nown-see-**a**-shuhn), and misspell it with an -**ou**-, *pron***ou***nciation*. Both of these may have logic on their side, since the verb is **pronounce**. But here, as so often, actual usage contradicts logic, and in standard English only **pronunciation** is acceptable.

prophecy, prophesy

The words **prophesy** and **prophecy** are often confused. **Prophesy** is the spelling that should be used for the verb (*he was prophesying a bumper harvest*), whereas **prophecy** is the correct spelling for the noun (*a bleak prophecy of war and ruin*).

prosciutto

You pronounce this Italian word /pruh-**shoo**-toh/. The correct way to spell it is with the letter **i** before the **u**, not the other way round, as often seen on menus. It may help to recollect the right order if you remember that in *fascist*, another Italian word, the same combination of letters -**sci**- is also pronounced as a **sh** sound.

P

prospective

Prospective is an adjective describing a likely future event or situation, as in *prospective students*, and *prospective changes in the law*. For its use in phrases where **perspective** is the appropriate word, see PERSPECTIVE.

prove

For complex historical reasons **prove** developed two past participles: **proved** and **proven**. Until recently, in British English **proved** was generally used for the past participle, and **proven** survived only in dialect, particularly in the Scottish legal phrase

not proven (usually pronounced /**proh**-v'n/), and adjectivally: *he has a proven track record* (generally pronounced /**proo**-v'n/). In the US, **proven** is much more common as the standard past participle than in Britain (*she has proven to be an outstanding manager*), but its use has been increasing recently in Britain; although this is perfectly correct, some traditionalists baulk at it.

purposely, purposefully

These are often confused, but in principle they mean somewhat different things. If you do something **purposely**, you do it on purpose, deliberately: *this administration purposely misled the American people*. If someone is **purposeful**, they are resolute and determined by nature. So, if they do something **purposefully**, they do it with great resolve and determination: *he got up and strode purposefully towards the trees*. To check if you are using the right word, try replacing it with *on purpose*. If you can replace it, as in the first example, then **purposely** is the right word to use.

queer

The word **queer** was first used to mean 'homosexual' in the 1920s. It was originally, and usually still is, a deliberately offensive and aggressive term when used by heterosexual people. In recent years, however, some gay people have taken the word and deliberately used it in place of *gay* or *homosexual*, in an attempt to deprive it of its negative power by using it positively. This use of **queer** is now well established and widely used among politically minded gay people (especially as an adjective or a noun modifier, as in *queer rights*) and at present it exists alongside the other, deliberately offensive use.

race

In recent years using the word **race** has become problematic because of the associations of the word with the racist ideologies and theories that grew out of the work of 19th-century anthropologists and physiologists. Although still used in general contexts, it is now often replaced by other words which are less emotionally charged, such as *people(s)* or *community*, as in *community relations*, and **racial** is often replaced by *ethnic*, as in *ethnic minority*.

rack

The relationship between the forms **rack** and **wrack** is complicated. The most common noun meaning of **rack**, 'a framework for holding and storing things', is always spelled **rack**, never **wrack**. The figurative meanings of the verb, deriving from the type of torture in which someone is stretched on a rack, can, however, be spelled either **rack** or **wrack**: *racked with guilt* or *wracked with guilt*; *rack your brains* or *wrack your brains*. In addition, the phrase **rack and ruin** can also be spelled **wrack and ruin**. In the contexts mentioned here as having the variant **wrack**, **rack** is always the commoner spelling.

random

The long-established meaning of **random** that everybody knows is 'done or happening without method or conscious decision': *here are some random thoughts*. The newer meaning, 'peculiar, strange, or unpredictable', can strike people above a certain age as novel and alien. As a result, it is still informal in tone. First appearing in the 1970s, it is now well established among people below a certain age, especially in the US: *you are so incredibly random*! In these two examples, **random** functions as an adjective. People also use it as a noun, to mean someone who is somewhere by chance, or who is not part of a particular group: *randoms are a fundamental ingredient at any good party*.

raring to do

This colourful, informal phrase means 'eager and enthusiastic to do something': *she was raring to get back to her work*. It is an American gift to our language. Some people say and write **rearing to do** something, which many people would consider wrong. But those who use **rearing** are in fact right to make the connection with the image of a rearing horse: **raring** is an American dialect form of **rearing**.

re

Some people claim that, strictly speaking, **re** should only be used in headings and references, as in *Re: Ainsworth versus Chambers*, but not as a normal word meaning 'about', as in *I saw the deputy head re the incident*. However, the evidence suggests that **re** is now widely used in the second way in official and semi-official contexts, and is now generally accepted. It is hard to see any compelling logical argument against using it as an ordinary English word in this way; it can, though, sound pretentious when used in everyday speech or writing, and *about* would probably serve better.

re-

In modern English, the tendency is for words formed with prefixes such as **re**- to be unhyphenated: **restore**, **remain**, **reacquaint.** One general exception to this is when the word to which **re**- attaches begins with **e**: in this case a hyphen is often inserted for clarity: **re-examine**, **re-enter**, **re-enact**. A hyphen is sometimes also used where the word formed with the prefix would be identical to an already existing word: **re-cover** (meaning 'cover again', as in *we decided to* re-cover *the dining-room chairs*) not **recover** (meaning 'get better in health'). Other prefixes such as **pre**- behave very similarly.

rearing to do

For the use of **rearing to do** to mean **raring to do**, see RARING TO DO.

r

reason

1 Some people object to statements like *the reason why I decided not to phone* on the grounds that what follows *the reason* should express a statement, using **that**, not imply a question with a **why**: *the reason that I decided not to phone* (or, more informally, *the reason I decided not to phone*).

2 Some people also object to the phrase *the reason ... is because*, as in *the reason I didn't phone is because my mother has been ill*. They object on the grounds that either *because* or *the reason* is unnecessary. It is supposedly better to use the word **that** instead (*the reason I didn't phone is that...*) or to rephrase altogether (*I didn't phone because...*).

Nevertheless, both the above usages are well established and, though more elegant phrasing can no doubt be found, they are generally accepted in standard English.

Red Indian

The term **Red Indian**, first recorded in the early 19th century, has largely fallen out of use, associated as it is with a historical period and the corresponding stereotypes of cowboys and Indians in the Wild West. If used today, the term may cause offence: the normal terms are now **American Indian** and **Native American** or, if appropriate, the name of the specific people (Cherokee, Iroquois, and so on).

reference

To **reference** something has a precise technical meaning in the field of bibliography, and a more general one. The technical meaning is 'to provide a book or article with citations for the sources of information mentioned', as in: *each chapter is referenced, citing literature up to 1990*. From this has developed a broader meaning of 'to mention or refer to': *one British Computer Society paper is referenced on page 35 of the White Paper*. Using the word in this somewhat broader way to mean that something is mentioned, often with a precise indication of where it is mentioned, is perfectly legitimate. But using it as a supposedly stylish replacement for the simpler **refer** or **mention**, as in *the media referenced our association in almost 40 articles*, may well irritate people alert to the nuances of language.

r

referendum

For information on which plural form to use, see LATIN PLURALS.

refute

The core meaning of **refute** is 'prove (a statement or theory) to be wrong', as in *attempts to refute Einstein's theory*. From the

1960s on, a more general meaning has developed from the core one, meaning simply 'deny', as in *I absolutely refute the charges made against me*. Traditionalists object to this second use but it is now widely accepted in standard English. However, it is wise to avoid it in writing for a more conservative audience.

regalia

The word **regalia** comes from Latin and is, technically speaking, the plural of the adjective *regalis*, meaning 'royal'. However, in the way the word is used in English today it behaves as a collective noun, similar to words like *staff* or *government*. This means that it can be used with either a singular or plural verb (*the regalia of Russian tsardom* ***is*** *now displayed in the Kremlin* or *the regalia of Russian tsardom* ***are*** *now displayed in the Kremlin*), but it has no other singular form. For more information, see NOUNS, SINGULAR AND PLURAL.

regard

See WITH REGARD TO.

register office

The form **register office** is the official term, but **registry office** is the form most often used in informal and non-official use.

regretfully, regrettably

The adjectives **regretful** and **regrettable** are distinct in meaning: **regretful** means 'feeling regret', as in *she shook her head with a regretful smile*, while **regrettable** means 'causing regret', as in *the loss of jobs is regrettable*. The adverbs **regretfully** and **regrettably** have not, however, preserved the same distinction. **Regretfully** is used as an adverb of manner to mean 'in a regretful manner' (*he sighed regretfully*), but is also used to mean 'it is regrettable that' (*regretfully, mounting costs forced the branch to close*). In this second use it stands in for **regrettably**. This use is now well established and is included in some modern dictionaries without comment.

reign, rein

The correct spelling of the idiomatic phrase is **a free rein**, not **a free reign**; see FREE REIN.

relative clauses

1 A **relative clause** is one that is connected to the main clause of the sentence by a word such as *who*, *whom*, *which*, *that*, and *whose*. The underlined part of the following sentence is a relative clause: *the items, which are believed to be family heirlooms, included a grandfather clock worth around £3,000.*

There are two types of relative clause: **defining** (or **restrictive**) **relative clauses** and **non-defining** (or **non-restrictive**) **relative clauses.**

- Defining relative clauses provide information which is essential to specify the noun or noun group to which they refer.
- Non-defining relative clauses give information which is additional and could be left out without affecting the meaning of the sentence.

Take the two sentences: *the books which were on the table are John's* and *the books, which were on the table, are John's.* In the first sentence the relative clause introduced by *which* uniquely identifies a specific group of books (the ones on the table) and states that they, and only they, are John's. In the second sentence the clause merely offers the additional information that John's books happen to be on the table; the fact that they are on the table does not distinguish them uniquely from other books which are not John's.

2 As you will see in the example above, defining clauses are not separated from the rest of the sentence, but non-defining clauses must be separated by commas. Ignoring this distinction can lead to unintentionally ▶

r

ambiguous or even comic effects. For example, the mistakenly defining relative clause in *if you are in need of assistance, please ask any member of staff who will be pleased to help* implies contrast with another set of staff who will not be pleased to help. A comma is needed before *who*.

3 Whether a relative clause is defining or non-defining also determines the choice between *that* and *which* when referring to things. If the clause is defining, either *that* or *which* can be used, e.g. *the coat that/which he had on yesterday was new* (we are identifying the coat by saying it is the one he had on yesterday, as opposed to any others he may have). However, in non-defining clauses, only *which* can be used: *that coat, which he had on yesterday, was made of pure alpaca and cost a bomb* (this is a coat we already know about and have referred to, and, by the way, he had it on yesterday). In the following example *that* should have been replaced by *which*: *the new edition of his book, that was first published in 2001, has proved even more successful than the first edition.*

relatively

The use of **relatively**, as in *it was relatively successful*, has been criticized on the grounds that there is no explicit comparison being made and that another word, such as *quite* or *rather*, would therefore be more appropriate. But even if no explicit comparison is being made **relatively** is often used in this way and is acceptable in standard English.

research

In British English, **research** is traditionally pronounced /ri-**serch**/, with the stress on the second syllable. In US English, the stress is reversed and comes on the first syllable: /**ree**-serch/. The US pronunciation is becoming more common in British

English and, although many people dislike it, it is now generally accepted as a standard variant of British English.

restaurateur

The word **restaurateur**, meaning a 'restaurant owner', comes directly from the French. The common misspelling *restauranteur*, copying the spelling of **restaurant** with an **n**, is found in nearly 10 per cent of uses of this word in the Oxford English Corpus.

restrictive relative clauses

See RELATIVE CLAUSES.

reverend

As a title, **Reverend** is used for members of the clergy; the traditionally correct way to refer to them is *the Reverend James Smith, the Reverend J. Smith*, or just *Mr Smith*, but not *Reverend Smith* or simply *Reverend*. On an envelope, for instance, especially where *Reverend* is abbreviated, *the* can be omitted: *Rev. J. Smith* or *Revd J. Smith*. Other words are prefixed in titles of more senior clergy: bishops are *Right Reverend*, archbishops are *Most Reverend*, and deans are *Very Reverend*, and these are treated similarly: *the Most Reverend Andrew Jones*; *Rt Rev. C. Brown*.

robust

Some words are, arguably, overused, and thus quickly become rather clichéd. **Robust** is one of them. In its meaning of 'uncompromising and forceful', it is a facile choice when someone is cornered and has to defend themselves, as in these two examples: *ministers were last night preparing a robust defence of Government economic performance; a rather more robust rebuttal of the allegations against her*. Synonyms which can deliver you from the tyranny of cliché include **assertive, forceful, forthright, rigorous,** and **vigorous.**

round

Round and **around** are interchangeable in some contexts, but not all. In many contexts in British English you can use either, as in *she put her arm round him; she put her arm around him*. There is, however, a general preference for **round** to be used for definite, specific movement (*she turned round; a bus came round the corner*), while **around** tends to be used in contexts which are less definite (*she wandered around for ages; costing around £3,000*) or for abstract uses (*a rumour circulating around the cocktail bars*).

In US English, the situation is different. The normal form in most contexts is **around**; **round** is generally regarded as informal or non-standard and is only standard in certain fixed expressions, as in *year-round* and *they went round and round in circles*.

rubbish

Rubbish used to be exclusively a noun, but in British English is now quite often used as a sort of adjective: *people might say I was a rubbish manager; she's rubbish at maths*. This use is still rather informal, and is best avoided in more formal writing.

's

There are a few special instances in which it is acceptable to use an apostrophe to indicate plurals, as with letters and symbols where the letter **s** added without punctuation could look odd or be undecipherable: *dot your i's and cross your t's; he rated a string of 9.9's from the jury*. However, in the formation of plurals of regular nouns it is incorrect to use an apostrophe, e.g. *six pens*, not *six pen's; oranges—6 for £1*, not *orange's—6 for £1*.

Sami

Sami is the term by which the **Lapps** themselves prefer to be known. Its use is becoming increasingly common, although **Lapp** is still the main term in general use.

sat

For the use of **sat** in sentences like *we were sat there for hours*, see SIT, STAND.

scarcely

Scarcely, like **barely**, should normally be followed by *when*, not *than*, to introduce a subsequent clause: *they had scarcely pulled to a halt when Rale flung the door open*.

scone

There are two possible pronunciations of the word **scone**: /skon/, rhyming with **gone**, and /skohn/, rhyming with **tone**. In US English /skohn/ is more common. In British English, the two pronunciations traditionally have different regional and class associations: /skon/ is standard in Scots, but in England tends to be associated with the north, and the northern working class, while /skohn/ is associated with the south and the middle class. In modern British English, however, the first pronunciation is increasingly common.

Scottish, Scot, Scots, Scotch

The terms **Scottish**, **Scot**, **Scots**, and **Scotch** are all variants of the same word. They have had different histories, however, and in modern English they have developed different uses and connotations. The normal everyday word used to mean 'of or relating to Scotland or its people' is **Scottish**, as in *Scottish people*; *Scottish hills*; *Scottish Gaelic*; or *she's English, not Scottish*. The normal, neutral word for 'a person from Scotland' is **Scot**, along with **Scotsman**, **Scotswoman**, and the plural form **the Scots** (or, less commonly, **the Scottish**). The word **Scotch**, meaning either 'of or relating to Scotland' or 'a person/the people from Scotland', was widely used in the past by Scottish writers such as Robert Burns and Sir Walter Scott, but it has become less common nowadays. It is detested by Scots (as being an 'English' invention) and is now uncommon in modern English, though occasionally used by unsuspecting American tourists. It only survives in certain fixed phrases, as for example *Scotch broth*, *Scotch egg*, *Scotch mist*, and *Scotch whisky*. **Scots** is used similarly to **Scottish**, as an adjective meaning 'of or relating to Scotland'. However, it tends to be used in a narrower meaning to refer specifically to the language spoken and used in Scotland, as in *a Scots accent* or *the Scots word for 'night'*.

seasonal

The words **seasonal** and **seasonable** are sometimes confused. **Seasonal** means 'relating to a particular season' (*seasonal fresh fruit*) or 'fluctuating or restricted according to the season' (*there are companies whose markets are seasonal*). **Seasonable** is a rather rare word which means 'usual for or appropriate to a particular season': *in December the magazine carried cartoons and songs, including a seasonable Christmas carol*.

sensual, sensuous

The words **sensual** and **sensuous** are frequently used interchangeably to mean 'gratifying the senses', especially in a sexual sense. Strictly speaking, this goes against a traditional distinction, by which **sensuous** is a more neutral term, meaning 'relating to the senses rather than the intellect', as in *swimming is a beautiful, sensuous experience*. **Sensual** relates to gratification of the senses, especially sexually, as in *a sensual massage*. In fact the word **sensuous** is thought to have been invented by Milton (1641) in a deliberate attempt to avoid the sexual overtones of **sensual**. In practice, the connotations are such that it is difficult to use **sensuous** in the non-sexual meaning. While traditionalists struggle to maintain a distinction, the evidence from the Oxford English Corpus and elsewhere suggests that the 'neutral' use of **sensuous** is rare in modern English. If a neutral meaning is intended it is advisable to find alternative wording.

sex

On the difference in use between the words **sex** and **gender**, see GENDER.

sexist language

It is very important to make sure that you do not unwittingly offend people by what might be considered sexist uses of language. Roughly since the 1970s, certain previously ▶

established uses of language have come to be regarded as discriminating against women, either because they are based on male terminology, e.g. *businessman*, or because women appear to be given a status that is linguistically and socially subsidiary, e.g. *actress*. Specific aspects of this are dealt with at the entries for **-ess**, **gender-neutral language**, **man**, and **-person**.

Different groups and individuals have different sensitivities to these issues, but there are some general guidelines that can be followed.

1 Where there is a choice between a word which specifies gender and a word which does not you should use the one which does not, unless the gender is relevant to the context. So, *chair* or *chairperson* is the gender-neutral word for the person running a meeting or a committee, as is *spokesperson* for someone who makes statements on behalf of a group or organization, and *head teacher* for someone in charge of a school. On the other hand, to say *she's a shrewd businessperson* rather than *she's a shrewd businesswoman* might sound somewhat forced. For more information see MAN.

2 In some cases the term which previously applied exclusively to males is used to refer to males and females, since the female form has negative connotations which the male does not. Accordingly, *actor*, *author*, *editor*, and *poet* are used irrespective of gender, e.g. *she is not only radiantly beautiful but a great actor*. For more information see -ESS.

3 When you are referring to groups of people in general, using words such as *each*, *everybody*, *anyone*, or nouns such as *individual*, *person*, *applicant*, *speaker*, and so forth, you should avoid using *he* or *his* to refer to them. Instead you can generally use *they* and *their*, and this use is perfectly acceptable nowadays, as in *each speaker will have their expenses reimbursed within one month of submitting* ▶

S

a claim. The alternatives to *they*, *their*, etc. are the rather cumbersome *he or she*, *his or hers*, etc. Invented forms such as *s/he* have not become established in general use. For more information see GENDER-NEUTRAL LANGUAGE.

4 When referring to the whole of humanity, phrases such as *the human race*, *humankind*, should be used instead of **mankind**. For more information, see MAN.

shall

There is considerable confusion about when to use **shall** and when **will**. The traditional rule in standard British English is that **shall** is used with *I* and *we* (first-person pronouns) to form the future tense, while **will** is used with *you*, *he*, *she*, *it*, *they* (second and third persons), e.g. *I shall be late*; *she will not be there*. To express a strong determination to do something the traditional rule is that **will** is used with the first person, and **shall** with the second and third persons, e.g. *I* ***will*** *not tolerate this*; *you* ***shall*** *go to the ball*. In practice, however, **shall** and **will** are today used more or less interchangeably in statements (though not in questions). Because both **shall** and **will** are usually contracted in speaking (*we'll*, *she'll*, etc.), there is often no need to make a choice between **shall** and **will**. This has no doubt helped weaken the distinction. The interchangeable use of **shall** and **will** is an acceptable part of standard modern British and US English.

she

1 For a discussion of whether to say *I am older than she* or *I am older than her*, see PERSONAL PRONOUN and THAN.

2 The use of the pronoun **he** to refer to a person of unspecified sex, once quite acceptable, has become problematic in recent years and is now usually regarded as old-fashioned or sexist. One of the responses to this has been to use **she** in the way that **he** has been used, to refer to people in general, irrespective of gender, as in *only include your child if you know she won't distract you*. In some types of writing, for example

books on childcare or child psychology, use of **she** has become quite common. In most contexts, however, it is likely to be distracting in the same way that **he** now is, and alternatives such as *he or she* or *they* are preferable. See also GENDER-NEUTRAL LANGUAGE.

sheer

The two verbs **sheer** and **shear** have a similar origin but do not have identical meanings. **Sheer**, the less common verb, means 'to swerve or change course quickly', as in *the boat sheers off the bank*. **Shear**, on the other hand, usually means 'to cut the wool off (a sheep)' and can also mean 'to break off (usually as a result of structural strain)', as in *the pins broke and the wing part sheared off*.

sherbet

The tendency to insert an **r** into the second syllable of **sherbet** is common; this misspelling happens in around 10 per cent of the uses of **sherbet** in the Oxford English Corpus.

should

1 As with *shall* and *will*, there is confusion about when to use **should** and **would**. The traditional rule is that **should** is used with first person pronouns (*I* and *we*), as in *I said I should be late*, and **would** is used with second and third persons (*you*, *he*, *she*, *it*, *they*), as in *you didn't say you would be late*. In practice, **would** is normally used instead of **should** in reported speech and conditional clauses: *I said I would be late*; *if we had known we would have invited her*. In spoken and informal contexts the issue rarely arises, since the distinction is obscured by the use of the contracted forms *I'd*, *we'd*, etc. In modern English, uses of **should** are dominated by the meanings relating to obligation (for which **would** cannot be substituted), as in *you should go out more often*, and for related emphatic uses, as in *you should have seen her face!*

2 For the use of **should of** instead of **should have**, see HAVE.

S

sight

On the confusion of **sight** and **site**, see SITE.

similar

The standard construction for **similar** is with **to**, as in *I've had problems similar to yours*. However, in British English, the construction **similar as** is sometimes used instead, as in *I've had similar problems* as *yourself*. This is not accepted as correct in standard English.

simplistic

Simplistic is first recorded in its modern meaning as recently as the 19th century. It differs from **simple** in implying a simplicity that is excessive or misleading rather than direct and useful: *'If you don't like what's on TV, just turn it off' is a simplistic remedy*.

sink

Historically, the past tense of **sink** has been both **sank** and **sunk** (*the boat sank; the boat sunk*), and the past participle has been both **sunk** and **sunken** (*the boat had already sunk; the boat had already sunken*). In modern standard English, however, the correct past is **sank** and the past participle is always **sunk**.

sit

Using **sat** (the past participle of **sit**) instead of **sitting** in such statements as *we were sat there for hours* is considered non-standard and dialectal by some people. It should be avoided in formal writing, but is acceptable and widely used when speaking in British (though not in US) English. See also STAND.

site

Confusion can arise between the words **site** and **sight**. As a noun, **site** means 'a place where something is constructed or has occurred' (*the site of the battle*; *the concrete is mixed on site*), while **sight** chiefly means 'the faculty or power of seeing' (*he lost his sight as a baby*).

skulduggery

This rather colourful-sounding word, deriving from the Scottish word **skulduddery**, ultimately has nothing to do with skulls, and was originally spelled with only one **l**. However, through a process of FOLK ETYMOLOGY, the spelling most commonly used these days is with **-ll-**, though strictly speaking this is incorrect.

slow

The word **slow** is normally used as an adjective (*a slow learner*; *the journey was slow*). It is also used as an adverb in certain specific contexts, including compounds such as *slow-acting* and *slow-moving* and in the expression *go slow*. Other adverbial use is informal and usually regarded as non-standard, as for example in *he drives too slow* and *go as slow as you can*. In such contexts standard English uses **slowly** instead. The use of **slow** and **slowly** in this respect contrasts with the use of *fast*, which is completely standard in use as both an adjective and an adverb; there is no word 'fastly'.

smell

The past tense and past participle of **smell** are both either **smelled** or **smelt**, and both forms are equally correct. **Smelt** is slightly preferred in British English, and **smelled** in American.

sneak

The traditional standard past form of **sneak** is **sneaked** (*she sneaked round the corner*). An alternative past form, **snuck** (*she snuck past me*), arose in the US in the 19th century. Until very recently **snuck** was confined to US dialect use and was regarded as non-standard. However, in the last few decades its use has spread in the US, where it is now regarded as a standard alternative to **sneaked** in all but the most formal contexts. In the Oxford English Corpus, there are now three times more US citations for **snuck** than there are for **sneaked**, and there is evidence of **snuck** sneaking into British English in a big way too.

soon

In standard English, the phrase **no sooner** is followed by **than**, as in *we had no sooner arrived than we had to leave*. This is because **sooner** is a comparative, and comparatives are followed by **than** (*earlier than*; *better than*, and so on). It is incorrect to follow **no sooner** with **when** instead of **than**, as in *we had no sooner arrived when we had to leave*.

sort

The construction **these sort of**, as in *I don't want to answer these sort of questions*, is technically ungrammatical. This is because *these* is plural and needs to agree with a plural noun (in this case **sorts** rather than **sort**). The construction is undoubtedly common and has been used for hundreds of years, but is best avoided in formal writing. See also KIND.

spastic

The word **spastic** has been used in medical contexts since the 18th century. In the 1970s and 1980s it became a term of abuse, used mainly by schoolchildren and directed towards any person regarded as incompetent or physically uncoordinated. Nowadays, the use of the word, whether as a noun or as an adjective, is likely to cause offence, and it is preferable, in the medical sense, to use phrasing such as *a person with cerebral palsy* instead.

specially

On the differences between **specially** and **especially**, see ESPECIALLY.

speed

Which is the correct past of **speed**? **Speeded** or **sped**? When the meaning is 'to go fast', the past tense and past participle are **sped**: *the car sped past*; *by that time she had sped down the road*. But if the meaning is 'to break a speed limit'; or if the verb is followed by **up**, **speeded** is the appropriate form in British English. Typical examples are: *he often speeded to get there in time*; *the reform process needs to be speeded up*. In American English **sped** is often used also in the second type of context, but sounds markedly odd to British ears.

spell

The form for the past tense and past participle is **spelt** or **spelled**. **Spelt** is more usual in British English, especially in the primary meaning 'to write or name the letters of a word'; **spelled** is more common in American English and in the phrasal verb **spell out**, meaning 'explain in detail'.

spill

The forms for the past tense and past participle are either **spilled** or **spilt**, and are equally correct. However, **spilled** is used much more often for both forms. There is no evidence of American and British usage being different.

spinster

The development of the word **spinster** is a good example of the way in which a word acquires unfavourable connotations to such an extent that it can no longer be used in a neutral way. From the 17th century the word was put after names as the official legal description of an unmarried woman: *Elizabeth Harris of London, Spinster*. This type of use survives today in some legal and religious contexts, as in the often humorously used *spinster of this parish*. In modern everyday English, however, **spinster** cannot be used to mean simply 'unmarried woman'; it is now always a derogatory term, conjuring up a stereotype of an older woman who is unmarried, childless, prissy, and repressed.

split infinitive

You have to really watch him; *to boldly go where no man has gone before*. It is still widely held that it is wrong to split infinitives—separate the infinitive marker **to** from the verb, as in the above examples. The dislike of split infinitives is long-standing but is not well founded, being based on an analogy with Latin. In Latin, infinitives consist of only one word (e.g. *crescere* 'to grow'; *amare* 'to love'), which makes them impossible to split: therefore, so the argument goes, they should not be split in

English either. But English is not the same as Latin. In particular, the placing of an adverb in English is extremely important in giving the appropriate emphasis: *you really have to watch him* and *to go boldly where no man has gone before*, examples where the infinitive is not split, either convey a different emphasis or sound awkward. Nowadays, some traditionalists may continue to consider the split infinitive an error in English. However, in standard English the principle of allowing split infinitives is broadly accepted as both normal and useful.

spoil

The forms for the past tense and past participle are either **spoiled** or **spoilt**, and are equally correct. However, there is a difference between American and British usage in that the spelling **spoilt** is rarely used in the US for either the past tense or the past participle, but in Britain it is as common as **spoiled** for the past participle, e.g. *we've been spoilt in recent years.*

spring

In British English the standard past tense is **sprang** (*she* sprang *forward*), while in US English the past can be either **sprang** or **sprung** (*I* sprung *out of bed*).

squaw

Until relatively recently, the word **squaw** was used neutrally in anthropological and other contexts to mean 'an American Indian woman or wife'. With changes in the political climate in the second half of the 20th century, however, the derogatory attitudes of the past towards American Indian women have meant that in modern North American English the word cannot be used in any context without being offensive. In British English the word has not acquired offensive connotations to the same extent, but it is nevertheless uncommon here too and now regarded as old-fashioned.

stand

Using **stood** (the past participle of **stand**) instead of **standing** in such statements as *my husband was stood on the other side of*

S

the fence is considered non-standard and dialectal by some people. It should be avoided in formal writing, but is acceptable and widely used when speaking. See also SIT.

stationary

The words **stationary** and **stationery** are often confused. **Stationary** is an adjective which means 'not moving or not intended to be moved', as in *a car collided with a stationary vehicle*, whereas **stationery** is a noun which means 'writing and other office materials', as in *I wrote to my father on the hotel stationery*. Around five per cent of the uses of **stationary** in the Oxford English Corpus are incorrect.

stood

For the use of **stood** in sentences like *we were stood there for hours*, see STAND.

stratum

In Latin, the word **stratum** is singular and its plural form is **strata**. In English, this distinction is maintained. It is therefore incorrect to use **strata** as a singular or to create the form *stratas* as the plural: a series of *overlying strata* not *a series of overlying stratas*, and a *new stratum was uncovered* not *a new strata was uncovered*. For further examples, see NOUNS, SINGULAR AND PLURAL.

subscribe

For the mistaken use of **ascribe** to to mean **subscribe to**, see ASCRIBE.

subjunctive

1 The **subjunctive** is a form of the verb expressing a wish or hypothesis in contrast to fact. It usually denotes what is imagined, wished, demanded, or proposed, as in the following examples: *I wish I were ten years younger; if I were you; the report recommends that he face* ▶

the tribunal; it is important that they be aware of the provisions of the Act.

2 The subjunctive is a legacy of Old English. It was common until about 1600, then went into decline, being retained in certain structures, such as following *if* or *as if*, and in certain fossilized phrases such as *as it were, be that as it may, come what may, far be it from me, God save the Queen, heaven forbid, perish the thought, so be it*, etc.

3 In modern English the subjunctive can be distinguished from the ordinary (indicative) form of the verb only in the third person singular present tense, which omits the final **s** (*God save the Queen*), and in the verb 'to be' (*I wish I were* and *it is important that they be aware*). It is regarded in many contexts as optional, and using it tends to convey a more formal tone.

4 The subjunctive has become very common, following American usage, in *'that'* clauses after verbs such as *demand, insist, pray, recommend, suggest*, and *wish*: *fundamentalist Islam decrees that men and women be strictly segregated; she insisted Jane sit there; it was suggested he wait till the next morning*. For more conservative British writers this use still has a distinctly transatlantic feel; in all cases it can be replaced by a construction with *should*, e.g. *it was suggested that he should wait till the next morning*. See also LEST.

5 Another area where usage seems to be changing is in phrases such *as if I were you, if it were up to me*, etc. People often say *if I was you* and *if it was up to me*, but the subjunctive is preferable in writing.

S

substitute

Traditionally, the verb **substitute** is followed by **for** and means 'to put (someone or something) in place of another', as in *she substituted the fake vase for the real one*. From the late 17th century on, **substitute** has also been used with **with** or **by** to mean 'replace (something) with something else', as in *she substituted the real vase with the fake one*. This can be confusing, since the two sentences shown above mean the same thing, yet the object of the verb and the object of the preposition have swapped over. Despite the potential confusion, the second, newer use is well established, especially in some scientific contexts, and though still disapproved of by traditionalists is now generally regarded as part of normal standard English.

suffice it to say

The traditional form of this phrase includes the word **it**: *suffice it to say he was not pleased*. However, the winds of change are buffeting this little word clean away, so that nowadays it is just as common to hear and see **suffice to say**. Nearly half of the examples in the Oxford English Corpus are in that form. The way the original phrase has been whittled down is an interesting example of how people can change English forever by being economical with words; see also AS FAR AS.

sulphur

In general use the standard British spelling is **sulphur** and the standard US spelling is **sulfur**. In chemistry, however, the **-f-** spelling is now the standard form in all related words in the field in both British and US contexts.

superior

S

When you compare two things, you normally link them with the word **than**: *my brother is older than me*. But **superior** is an exception to this rule. You use the word **to** instead: *restaurant industry managers consider US beef to be superior to Canadian and Australian beef*. A second difference between superior and other adjectives is that you cannot put the word **more** in front of it. So, it is correct to say *A is far superior to B*, and wrong to say *A* is *far more superior to B*.

supersede

The standard spelling is **supersede** rather than *supercede*. The word is derived from the Latin verb *supersedere* but has been influenced by the presence of other words in English spelled with a **c**, such as *intercede* and *accede*. The **c** spelling is recorded as early as the 16th century but is still generally regarded as incorrect and should be avoided in any kind of formal writing.

swim

In standard English, the past tense of **swim** is **swam** (*she swam to the shore*) and the past participle is **swum** (*she had never swum there before*). In the 17th and 18th centuries **swam** and **swum** were used interchangeably for the past participle, but this is not acceptable in standard modern English.

syllabus

Both **syllabuses** and **syllabi** are correct as plurals of **syllabus**, though in speech the first will sound more natural, the second slightly academic. For more guidance on words with more than one plural, see LATIN PLURALS.

sympathy

On the difference between **sympathy** and **empathy**, see EMPATHY.

tableau

Tableau comes from French, and is singular in meaning. The plural in English and French is **tableaux**. It is therefore incorrect to use **tableaux** in sentences such as *his pictures are a tableaux of military life behind the front line*. For further examples of this kind of mistake, see NOUNS, SINGULAR AND PLURAL.

text

At the moment there seems to be no agreement on which is the 'correct' form for the verb **text** in the past tense: **text** or **texted**. **Text**, as in *I text you but you didn't reply* is often heard, but **texted** is also used, and is found in writing. If to **text** is a regular verb, like *love*, then **texted** is the correct past tense and participle. However, people may be treating it as an irregular verb, like *put*, with the same past form as the present, perhaps influenced by the fact that **text** sounds like a past participle, as though it were 'texed'. It will be interesting to see which form wins out in the long run.

than

Traditionalists hold that personal pronouns following **than** should be in the subjective rather than the objective case: *he is smaller than she* rather than *he is smaller than her*. This argument is based on analysing **than** as a conjunction, with the personal pronoun ('she') standing in for a full clause: *he is smaller* ***than she is***. However, many would argue that **than** in this context is not a conjunction but a preposition, grammatically similar to words like *with*, *between*, and *for*. If it is a preposition, the personal pronoun is objective: *he is smaller than her* is standard, in just the same way as, for example, *I work with her* is standard (not *I work with she*). Whatever the grammatical analysis, the evidence confirms that sentences like *he is smaller than she* are uncommon in modern English and only ever found in formal contexts. In speech they would certainly sound affected or pompous. Uses involving the objective personal pronoun, on the other hand, are almost universal. For more explanation, see PERSONAL PRONOUN and BETWEEN.

thankfully

Thankfully has been used for centuries to mean 'in a thankful manner', as in *she accepted the offer thankfully*. Since the 1960s it has also been used to mean 'fortunately', as in *thankfully, we didn't have to wait*. Although this use has not attracted the same amount of attention as **hopefully**, it has been criticized for the same reasons. It is, however, far commoner now than the traditional use, accounting for more than 80 per cent of uses of **thankfully** in the Oxford English Corpus. For further explanation, see HOPEFULLY.

that

1 The word **that** can be omitted in standard English where it introduces a subordinate clause, as in *she said (that) she was satisfied*. It can also be dropped in a defining relative clause where the subject of the subordinate clause is not the same as the subject of the main clause, as in *the book (that) I've just written* ('the book' and 'I' are two different subjects). Where the subject of the subordinate clause and the main clause are the same, use of the word **that** is obligatory, as in *the woman that owns the place* ('the woman' is the subject of both clauses).

2 It is sometimes argued that, in defining relative clauses, **that** should be used for non-human references, while **who** should be used for human references: *a house that overlooks the park* but *the woman who lives next door*. In practice, although it is true to say that **who** is restricted to human references, the function of **that** is flexible. It has been used for human and non-human references since at least the 11th century. In standard English it is interchangeable with **who** in this context.

3 People are often unsure whether there is any difference between the use of **that** and **which** in sentences such as *any book that gets children reading is worth having* and *any book which gets children reading is worth having*. The general rule is that in defining relative clauses, where the relative clause serves to define or restrict the reference to the particular thing or person described, **which** can replace **that**, as in the example just given. However, in non-defining relative clauses, where the relative clause serves only to give additional information, **that** cannot be used: *this book, which is set in the last century, is very popular with teenagers* but not *this book, that is set in the last century, is very popular with teenagers*. In US English it is usually recommended that **which** should be used only for non-defining relative clauses.

thee

The word **thee** is still used in some traditional dialects (e.g. in northern England) and among certain religious groups, but in standard English it is restricted to archaic contexts. For more details see THOU.

their

1 Do not confuse **their** and **there**. **Their** means 'belonging to them', while **there** means principally 'in/to that place', as in *almost 3,000 people made their living there*.

2 On the use of **their** to mean 'his or her', see THEY.

theirs

1 There is no need for an apostrophe in **theirs**.

2 On the use of **theirs** to mean 'his or hers', see THEY.

them

On the use of **them** in the singular to mean 'him or her', see THEY.

themself

1 The standard reflexive form corresponding to *they* and *them* is **themselves**, as in *they can do it themselves*. The singular form **themself**, first recorded in the 14th century, has re-emerged in recent years corresponding to the singular gender-neutral use of *they*, as in *this is the first step in helping someone to help* themself. The form is not widely accepted in standard English, however. Compare OURSELF.

2 On the use of **themselves** to mean 'himself or herself', see THEY.

thence

Thence and **from thence** are both used to mean 'from a place or source previously mentioned', as in *they intended to cycle on into France and thence home via Belgium*; *this is not a commodity which can be transported from thence*. Some traditionalists maintain that 'from' in **from thence** is unnecessary, since the word already contains the idea of 'from', so that effectively you are saying 'from from there.'

thesaurus

Thesaurus is pronounced /thi-**saw**-ruhs/, emphasizing the second syllable. Both **thesauruses** and **thesauri** are correct as plurals, though in speech the first will sound more natural, the second somewhat academic. For more guidance on words with alternative plural forms, see LATIN PLURALS.

they

The word **they** has been used since at least the 16th century as a singular pronoun to refer to a person of unspecified sex (and its counterparts **them**, **their**, **theirs**, and **themselves** have been used similarly). In the late 20th century, as the traditional use of **he** to refer to a person of either sex came under scrutiny on the grounds of sexism, this use of **they** became more common. It is now generally accepted in contexts where it follows an indefinite pronoun such as *anyone*, *no one*, or *someone* or a noun used to refer generally to males and females, such as *person*, *student*, *applicant*, *employee*, etc., as in ***anyone*** *can join if* ***they*** *are a resident*, ***each*** *to* ***their*** *own*, ***any student*** *using these facilities* ***is*** *responsible for their belongings*. The use of **they** after singular nouns is now common, though less widely accepted, especially in formal contexts. Sentences such as *ask* ***a friend*** *if* ***they*** *could help* are still criticized by some for being ungrammatical. Nevertheless, in view of the growing acceptance of **they** and its obvious practical advantages, this use after a noun is now an established pattern in English. Where you wish to avoid it, you can often do so by rewriting the whole sentence in the plural: ***any student*** *using these facilities* ***is*** *responsible for their belongings* can become ***any students*** *using these facilities* ***are*** *responsible for their belongings*.

thou

In modern English, the personal pronoun **you** (together with the possessives **your** and **yours**) covers a number of uses: it is both singular and plural, both objective and subjective, and both formal and familiar. This has not always been the case. In Old English and Middle English some of these different functions of **you** were supplied by different words. Thus, **thou** was at one time the singular subjective case (*thou art a beast*), while **thee** was the singular objective case (*he cares not for thee*). In addition, **thy** was equivalent to the modern *your*, and **thine** was equivalent to the modern *yours*: *in the sweat of thy brow shalt thou eat bread*; *for thine is the kingdom, the power, and the glory*. The forms **you** and **ye**, on the other hand, used always to mean more than one person. By the 19th century they had become universal in standard English for both singular and plural, polite and familiar. In present-day use, **thou**, **thee**, **thy**, and **thine** survive in some traditional dialects but otherwise are found only in archaic contexts.

though

Though and **although** are virtually interchangeable, the only difference being that **though** tends to be less formal than **although**.

thusly

First coined in the 19th century as a humorous form of **thus**, **thusly** is now quite commonly used in the meaning of 'in this way'. Many people consider it superfluous, and it should probably be avoided in writing. Compare IRREGARDLESS.

till

In most contexts, **till** and **until** have the same meaning and are interchangeable. The main difference is that **till** is generally considered to be the more informal of the two and occurs less frequently than **until** in writing. **Until** also tends to be the natural choice at the beginning of a sentence: until *very recently, there was still a chance of rescuing the situation*. Interestingly, although it is commonly assumed that **till** is an abbreviated form of **until** (the spellings *'till* and *'til* reflect this), **till** is in fact the earlier form. **Until** appears to have been formed by the addition of Old Norse *und* 'as far as' at least several hundred years after **till** was first used.

time

People are sometimes unsure about where to put the apostrophe in phrases such as *in a week's time*, or *in two years' time*. To help you decide if the apostrophe comes before or after the letter **s**, first try rephrasing the previous examples using the word **of**: *in the time of a week*, *in the time of two years*. Then look carefully at the final letter of the relevant word as it now appears. The correct place to put the apostrophe is immediately after that letter. Apply this method to the phrase you are unsure about, and you will not go wrong.

titivate

The verbs **titillate** and **titivate** sound alike but do not have the same meaning, and to use the wrong one could be unfortunate. **Titillate** is the commoner word and means 'to stimulate or excite', as in *the press are paid to titillate the public*. **Titivate**, on the other hand, means 'to adorn or smarten up', as in *she titivated her hair*.

toothcomb

If you have ever wondered what a **toothcomb** is, and why on earth anybody would want to comb their teeth, wonder no more. There is no such thing. The forms **toothcomb** and **fine toothcomb** come from a misreading of the noun **fine-tooth comb**, meaning a comb with very finely spaced teeth. In modern standard English the versions **finetooth comb** and **fine toothcomb** are largely acceptable, if implausible.

tortuous, torturous

Tortuous and **torturous** have different literal meanings. **Tortuous** means 'full of twists and turns'. **Torturous** is derived from **torture**, and means 'involving or causing torture'. A ***tortuous** route* is one that is twisting and winding, and a ***torturous** death* is one that is extremely painful. In their figurative meanings both words can mean 'difficult or complex', and it is in this sense that they overlap. A ***tortuous** judgement* is one that has many complicating features, and a ***torturous** judgement* is one that is painfully difficult to make. **Tortuous** is used more often to express this meaning of 'difficult or complex', and is the better and more accurate choice. The overlap in meaning also occasionally leads to **tortuous** being used incorrectly for **torturous**, as in *my family, for whom this has been a tortuous ordeal, have been a tower of strength*.

transpire

The standard general meaning of **transpire** is 'to come to be known' as in *it transpired that Mark had been baptized a Catholic*. From this a looser sense has developed, meaning 'to happen or occur': *I'm going to find out exactly what transpired*. This looser sense is first recorded in US English in the late 18th century, and was listed in US dictionaries from the 19th century onwards. It is often criticized for being jargon, or for being unnecessarily long when *occur* and *happen* would do perfectly well. The newer meaning is very common, however, and generally accepted in most contexts, except by purists.

treason

Formerly, there were two types of crime to which the term **treason** was applied: **petty treason**, the crime of murdering one's master, and **high treason**, the crime of betraying one's country. The crime of petty treason was abolished in 1828 and in modern use high treason is now often simply called **treason**.

tribe

In historical contexts, the word **tribe** is broadly accepted (*the area was inhabited by Slavic tribes*). However, in contemporary contexts, used to refer to a community living within a traditional society today, the word is problematic. It is strongly associated with past attitudes of white colonialists towards so-called primitive or uncivilized peoples living in remote, undeveloped places. For this reason, it is generally preferable to use alternative terms such as *community*, *nation*, or *people*.

-trix

The suffix **-trix** has been used since the 15th century to form feminine agent nouns corresponding to masculine forms ending in **-tor**. Although a wide variety of forms have been coined, few of them have ever had wide currency. In modern use the suffix is found chiefly in legal terms such as *executrix*, *administratrix*, and *testatrix* but also in the word *dominatrix*.

try and

Some people consider it is incorrect to use **try and** plus an infinitive in sentences such as *we should try and help them*, and suggest that *we should try to help them* is the only correct form. In practice there is little discernible difference in meaning, although there is a difference in formality, with **try to** being regarded as more formal than **try and**. The construction **try and** is grammatically odd, however, in that it cannot be used if **try** has the form **tries**, **tried**, or **trying**. So, for example, sentences like *she tried and fix it*, *she tried and fixed it*, and *they are trying and renew their visa* are not acceptable, while their equivalents *she tried to fix it* and *they are trying to renew their visa*, as well as *try and get over it* and *it is vital that they try and come*, undoubtedly are. For this reason **try and** is best regarded as a fixed idiom used only in its infinitive and imperative form.

Two words or one

The spelling of English words is not fixed forever, and changes over time. We no longer spell **pathetic** as *pathetick* with a final **k** as Doctor Johnson did, and we put a letter **b** in **doubt**, even though no one did before the 15th century. Similarly, a number of common words in English started out as two-word phrases which always functioned as single ▶

units of meaning and eventually became fused in a single word, such as **forever**, **somebody**, or **everyone**.

As regards writing words in single units or separately, in current English there are two tendencies worth commenting on. On the one hand there is a tendency to join together fixed expressions which have for a long time been written separately, e.g. **thankyou** for **thank you** and **straightaway** for **straight away**. This trend continues the well-established process which fused **for** and **ever** into **forever**, and **some** and **body** into **somebody**, and it is probably more likely if there is a direct analogy with an existing word: **anymore** is analogous to **anyone** and **anybody**.

On the other hand, an opposite process can also be observed with a very limited group of words: some people write as individual words terms such as **nonetheless** which are standardly written as a single word.

Of the two trends, the first appears to be much the stronger. For instance, in the Oxford English Corpus, the phrase **some time** now appears as **sometime** in 32 per cent of all cases in American English and 19 per cent of all cases in British English: *we really want to do a live record sometime*.

The move towards writing fixed expressions as one word is stronger in American than in British English. For instance, in American English **someday** has now become more or less standard, and **anymore** and **underway** look set to follow. Although the same trend is apparent in British English, it lags behind. The one exception is **thankyou**, which, relative to **thank you**, is more common in British than American English.

Fused forms almost always emerge first in informal English, used in contexts such as chatrooms and weblogs, and are slower to spread to more formal, edited text such as newspapers and magazines. In formal British English it is therefore probably still best to avoid most of them.

The shift towards writing single words as their component parts is far less strong: in the Oxford English Corpus ▶

nonetheless is written as **none the less** in 6 per cent of cases. We will have to wait and see whether it becomes more prevalent in the future, but for the time being writing such words this way will generally be considered mistaken in formal written English. See also ALBEIT, AWHILE, EVERYDAY, EVERYONE, HOWEVER, WHATEVER, WHENEVER, WHEREVER, WORTHWHILE.

un-

The prefixes **un-** and **non-** both mean 'not', but there is often a distinction in emphasis. **Un-** tends to be stronger and less neutral than **non-**: consider the differences between *unacademic* and *non-academic*, as in *his language was refreshingly unacademic* (i.e. not obscure and full of technical argon); *a non-academic life suits him* (i.e. a life in which he does not have to study or teach).

uncharted, unchartered

People sometimes wrongly use **unchartered** instead of **uncharted** in phrases such as *the uncharted waters of the Indian Ocean* or *uncharted territory*. To avoid this mistake it is helpful to remember that the image suggested is that of going into unexplored—literally or figuratively—places that have not been mapped. A **chart** is a kind of map used by navigators, hence the image of **uncharted**.

unexceptionable, unexceptional

There is a clear distinction in meaning between **exceptionable** ('open to objection') and **exceptional** ('out of the ordinary; very good'). However, this distinction has become blurred in the negative forms **unexceptionable** and **unexceptional**. Strictly speaking, **unexceptionable** means 'not open to objection', as in *this view is unexceptionable in itself*, while **unexceptional** means 'not out of the ordinary; usual', as in *the hotel was adequate but unexceptional*. But, although the distinction may be clear in these two examples, the meaning of **unexceptionable** is often indeterminate between 'not open to objection' and 'ordinary', as in *the food was bland*

and unexceptionable or *the candidates were pretty unexceptionable.*

uninterested

On the difference between **uninterested** and **disinterested**, see DISINTERESTED.

unique

There is a set of adjectives, including *unique*, *complete*, *equal*, *infinite*, and *perfect*, whose core meanings are absolute. Therefore, according to a traditional argument, they cannot be modified by adverbs such as *really*, *quite*, *almost*, or *very*. For example, since the core meaning of **unique** (from Latin 'one') is 'being only one of its kind', it is logically impossible, the argument goes, to modify it with an adverb: it either is 'unique' or it is not, and there are no in-between stages. In practice, however, these adjectives are so commonly modified by *quite*, *almost*, etc. that such uses go unnoticed by most people and must by now be considered standard English.

United Kingdom

See BRITAIN.

unlike

The use of **unlike** as a conjunction, as in *she was behaving unlike she'd ever behaved before*, is not considered standard English. It can be avoided by using **as** or **in a way that** with a negative instead: *she was behaving* as *she'd never behaved before*; *we do it* in a way that *isn't pushy or overtly political*.

unsociable, unsocial

u

There is some overlap in the use of the adjectives **unsociable**, **unsocial**, and **antisocial**, but they also have distinct core meanings. Generally speaking, **unsociable** means 'not enjoying the company of others', as in *Terry was grumpy and unsociable*. It can also mean 'not conducive to friendly social relations', as in *surfing the Net is an unsociable habit*. **Antisocial** means 'contrary to the laws and customs of a society', as in *aggressive and antisocial behaviour*. **Unsocial** is usually only used to describe hours 'falling outside the normal working day', as in *employees were expected to work unsocial hours*. It is therefore incorrect to use it in phrases such as *violence and unsocial behaviour*.

unthaw

Logically, the verb **unthaw** should mean 'freeze', but in North America it means exactly the same as **thaw** (as in *the warm weather helped unthaw the rail lines*); because of the risk of confusion it is not part of standard usage. **Unthawed** as an adjective always means 'still frozen', but it is best avoided because many contexts may be ambiguous.

until

On the differences between **until** and **till**, see TILL.

untouchable

In meanings relating to the traditional Hindu caste system, the term **untouchable** and the social restrictions accompanying it were declared illegal in the constitution of India in 1949 and of Pakistan in 1953. The official term for 'untouchables' today is **the Scheduled Castes**.

upmost

Upmost is a somewhat rare adjective and a variant of **uppermost**. It refers to the position of something, as in *the upmost layer*. Through a process of FOLK ETYMOLOGY it is sometimes incorrectly used instead of **utmost**: e.g. *with the upmost care*, instead of *with the utmost care*; *to do your upmost*, instead of *to do your utmost*.

upon

The preposition **upon** has the same core meaning as the preposition **on**. However, in modern English **upon** tends to be restricted to more formal contexts or to established phrases and idioms, such as *once upon a time* and *row upon row of empty seats*.

us

People are often unsure whether it is correct to say *they are richer* ***than us***, or *they are richer* ***than we*** (or ***than we are***). For a discussion of this topic see PERSONAL PRONOUN AND THAN.

use

1 The construction **used to**, as in *we used to replace the picture tubes in our television sets when they failed*, is standard English, but difficulties arise with the formation of negatives and questions. Traditionally, they are formed without the auxiliary verb *do*, as in *it* ***used not to*** *be like that* and ***used*** *she* ***to*** *come here?* In modern English this question form is now regarded as very formal or old-fashioned, and the construction with *do* is broadly accepted as standard, as in ***did*** *they* ***use to*** *come here?* Negative constructions with *do*, on the other hand (as in *it* ***didn't use to*** *be like that*), though common, are informal and are not generally accepted.

2 There is sometimes confusion over whether to use the form **used to** or **use to**, which has arisen largely because the pronunciation is the same in both cases: /**yoos** too/. Except in negatives and questions, the correct form is **used to**: *we used to go to the cinema all the time*, not *we use to go to the cinema all the time*. However, in negatives and questions using the auxiliary verb *do*, the correct form is **use to**, because the form of the verb required is the infinitive: *I didn't use to like mushrooms*, not *I didn't used to like mushrooms*.

utmost

For the occasional confusion between **upmost** and **utmost**, see UPMOST.

u
v

various

In standard English the word **various** is normally used as an adjective, e.g. *dresses of* various *colours*. It is sometimes also used as a pronoun followed by *of*, as in *various of her friends had called*. Although this use is similar to that of words such as *several* and *many* (e.g. *several of her friends had called*), it is sometimes regarded as incorrect.

venal, venial

Venal and **venial** are sometimes confused. **Venal** means 'bribable, corrupt', as in *venal consulate officials have reportedly swindled untold thousands*, whereas **venial** is used to refer to a sin or offence that is excusable or pardonable, as opposed to a *mortal* sin: *a venial sin*, *a venial mistake*.

verbal

Some people claim that the true meaning of the adjective **verbal** is 'of or concerned with words', whether spoken or written (as in *verbal abuse*), and that it should not be used to mean 'spoken rather than written' (as in *a verbal agreement*). For this meaning it is said that the adjective **oral** should be used instead. In practice, however, **verbal** is well established in this meaning and in certain idiomatic phrases (such as *a verbal agreement*) cannot be simply replaced by **oral**.

verbs formed from nouns

English is remarkably free-and-easy in the way it can use the same word in many different grammatical functions. A very common word like *down* can be used as an adverb, preposition, adjective, verb, or noun, as in *she looked down*; *I walked down the stairs*; *he's been so down lately*; *he downed his drink*; *she had a real down on Angela*; conjunctions can become nouns, as in *too many ifs and buts*; proper nouns can be used as adjectives, as in *a very Hollywood view of life*, and so forth. Yet despite this grammatical freedom there is one particular process of forming new words which often offends purists and traditionalists: forming verbs from nouns.
The name by which this process is known, **verbing**, first recorded as long ago as 1757, is, appropriately, an example of this selfsame process, since it derives from a noun.
For whatever reason, many people object to the creation of new words in this way. There is a story from a while ▶

V

back that an American wished to contact an Oxford don, to which the reply was: 'I am delighted that you have arrived in Oxford. The verb "to contact" has not.' Yet respectable and well-thought-of verbs have for several centuries been formed from nouns (and occasionally adjectives) by these methods:

- by using exactly the same word (e.g. *to question*, *to knife*, *to quiz*, *to service*)
- by adding a suffix such as *-ize* (*to prioritize*, *to randomize*)
- by shortening the noun (*to edit*, *to diagnose*, *to televise*)

Nobody objects to *pepper* as in *his conversation was peppered with risqué anecdotes*, or to *floor* as in *his question floored me*.

It might be some people's aversion to new words in general that puts them off these formations; or they might be put off by the fact that many of them come from the mistrusted worlds of business and politics, and so have a feeling of jargon. Whatever the reason, there is no doubt that **verbing** is a very productive process and will continue to add new words to English. Below are a few more examples of recent and not so recent words, together with their first date, if known, in that meaning.

to access	to gain access to	1962
to author	to write	1940
chipmunking	keying frenetically on a mobile phone while in the middle of another activity, such as a meeting	
to contact	to get in touch with	1929
to enthuse	to fill with enthusiasm	1827
to interface	to interact	1967
to offshore	to move a business operation abroad	1987
to podcast	to put audio files on the Internet for downloading	

waive, waiver, wave, waver

Waive is sometimes confused with **wave**. **Waive** means 'not to insist on', as in *he will waive all rights to the money* or *her fees would be waived*, whereas the much more common word **wave** means 'to move to and fro'. A **waiver** is the act of **waiving** a right or claim (or a document recording that) whereas **to waver** means mainly 'to falter' as in *her voice wavered*; *he never wavered in his resolve*.

was, were

On whether it is more correct to say *if I was a rich man* or *if I were a rich man*, etc., see the article on the SUBJUNCTIVE.

well

In many varieties of English, people below a certain age now quite commonly use **well** to emphasize any adjective: *she is well thick*; *Jack said he was well chuffed*; *this is a well cool bar*; *a technology now well familiar*. Using **well** like this is still markedly informal even in speech, and should be avoided in any kind of serious writing. It is, nevertheless, a logical extension of some old-established ways of using **well** for emphasis.

well-

1 The adverb **well** is often used in combination with past participles to form adjectival compounds: **well** *adjusted*, **well** *intentioned*, **well** *known*, and so on. As far as hyphenation is concerned, the general stylistic principle is that if the adjectival compound comes before the noun (i.e. when used attributively), it should be hyphenated (*a* **well**-*intentioned remark*) but that if it stands alone after the verb (i.e. when used predicatively), it should not be hyphenated (*her remarks were* **well** *intentioned*).

2 In combinations with **best**-, such as **best**-*built*, **best**-*dressed*, **best**-*intentioned*, **best**-*looking*, the hyphen is used irrespective of the position of the word, e.g. *the* **best**-*looking man I know, she's the* **best**-*looking of the whole clan*. See also HYPHENATION.

were, was

On whether it is more correct to say *if I was a rich man or if I were a rich man*, etc., see SUBJUNCTIVE.

whatever

In its emphatic use (e.g. *whatever was she thinking of?*) **whatever** can also written as two words (*what ever was she thinking of?*). In its other meanings, however, it must be written as one word, e.g. *do whatever you like*; *they received no help whatever*.

whence (also from whence)

Strictly speaking, **whence** means 'from what place', as in *whence did you come?* Accordingly, some people maintain that 'from' in **from thence** as in *from whence did you come?* is unnecessary, since the word already contains the idea of 'from', so that effectively you are saying 'from from where'. The use with *from* is very common, though, and has been used by reputable writers since the 14th century. It is now broadly accepted in standard English.

whenever

In its emphatic use (e.g. *whenever shall we arrive?*) the one-word form **whenever** may also be written as two words (*when ever shall we arrive?*). In its other meanings, however, it must be written as one word: *you can ask for help whenever you need it*; *I'll do it at the weekend or whenever*.

wherever

In its emphatic use (e.g. *wherever can he have got to?*) the one-word form **wherever** may also be written as two words (*where ever can he have got to?*). In its other meanings, however, it must be written as one word: *meet me wherever you like*; *it should be available wherever you shop*; *use wholegrain cereals wherever possible*.

W

whether

On the difference between **whether** and **if**, see IF.

which

On the differences between **which** and **that** in relative clauses, see THAT.

whichever

Whichever should always be written as one word, e.g. *you're safe with whichever option you choose*. However, do not confuse it with constructions in which the separate words *which* and *ever* quite legitimately come together, e.g. *this reminds me of the 5-year development plans, none of **which ever** worked*.

while

On the distinction between **worth while** and **worthwhile**, see WORTHWHILE. For **a while** versus **awhile,** see AWHILE.

white

The word **white** has been used to refer to the skin colour of Europeans or people of European extraction since the early 17th century. Unlike other labels for skin colour such as *red* or *yellow*, **white** has not been generally used in a derogatory way. In modern contexts there is a growing tendency to prefer terms which relate to geographical origin rather than skin colour: hence the current preference in the US for African American rather than *black* and European rather than *white*.

who, whom

1 There is a continuing debate in English usage about when to use **who** and when to use **whom**. According to formal grammar, **who** forms the subjective case and so should be used in subject position in a sentence, as in *who decided this?* The form **whom**, on the other hand, forms the objective case and so should be used in object position in a sentence, as in *whom do you think we should support?* (where it is the object of *support*); and after a ▶

preposition: *to whom do you wish to speak?* Although some people still use **who** and **whom** according to the rules of formal grammar as stated here, there are many more who rarely use **whom** at all; it has retreated steadily and is now largely restricted to formal contexts. So formal has it become, indeed, that the American humorist Calvin Triller observed, 'As far as I'm concerned, "whom" is a word that was invented to make everyone sound like a butler'.

2 The normal practice in modern English is to use **who** instead of **whom**: *who do you think we should support?*; *who do you wish to speak to?* In the second example, the preposition *to* is moved to the end of the sentence. Such uses are today broadly accepted in standard English, and in both the previous examples using **whom** could have sounded starchy and off-putting.

3 Many people use **whom** so rarely that when they do venture into these further reaches of grammar they use it inappropriately. The most common mistake made with **whom** is to use it to refer to the subject of the sentence: e.g. *a leader who has been linked to Al Qaeda and whom US officials have said is behind other attacks*. What has happened here is that **whom** has been used in the mistaken belief that it is the object of the verb *have said*, whereas it is the subject of the phrase *is behind other attacks*. It is very common for this mistake to be made after verbs such as *say*, *claim*, *suspect*, *think*, etc.

4 A second mistake, based on the correct notion that **whom** is the appropriate form after a preposition, is to use it when it is part of a complete clause introduced by a preposition, as in: *the camera is trained almost exclusively on one of the participants, regardless of whom is talking*. **Who** should be used here, as it is the subject of *is talking*.

5 On the use of **who** and **that** in relative clauses, see RELATIVE CLAUSES and THAT.

whoever

In the emphatic use (*whoever does he think he is?*) **whoever** can also be written as two words. In its other meanings, however, it must be written as one word: *whoever wins should be guaranteed an Olympic place*; *come out, whoever you are.*

whom

On the use of **who** and **whom**, see WHO.

who's

A common written mistake is to confuse **who's** with **whose**. The form **who's** represents a contraction of **who is** or **who has**, while **whose** is a possessive pronoun or determiner used in questions, as in *whose is this?* or *whose turn is it?*

why

On the phrase **the reason why**, see REASON.

will

On the differences in use between **will** and **shall**, see SHALL.

-wise

In modern English the suffix **-wise** is attached to nouns to form a sentence adverb meaning 'concerning or with respect to', as in *confidence-wise*, *tax-wise*, *price-wise*, *time-wise*, *news-wise*, and *culture-wise*. The suffix is very productive and widely used in modern English but many of the words so formed are considered inelegant or not good English style. If you want to avoid using **-wise**, the solution is often to omit the word entirely, or to recast the sentence. For instance, *we were late time-wise, but so was everyone else* is just as good without *time-wise*, while *until things get better business-wise* can be reworded as *until business gets better.*

W

wish

People say both *I wish I were rich* and *I wish I was rich*, but the second form is often viewed as incorrect. On this question, see SUBJUNCTIVE.

with regard to

The correct form of this phrase, meaning broadly 'about', is to use **regard** without a final **s**: *suspicion with regard to British intentions*. However, possibly because of the influence of the phrase *to give one's regards to someone*, people often say and write **with regards to**. It is best to avoid doing this in formal or academic writing, since many people are likely to consider it a mistake.

worthwhile

When the adjective **worthwhile** is used before the noun (i.e. attributively) it is always written as one word: *a worthwhile cause*. However, when it stands alone and comes *after* the verb (i.e. when used predicatively) it may be written as either one or two words: *we didn't think it was worthwhile* or *we didn't think it was worth while*.

would

1. On the differences in use between **would** and **should**, see SHOULD.
2. For a discussion of the use of **would of** instead of **would have**, see HAVE.

wrack

On the complicated relationship between **wrack** and **rack**, see RACK.

wreak

The past participle of **wreak** is **wreaked**, as in *boll weevils wreaked havoc on the US cotton industry*. An alternative expression is **wrought havoc**, as in *over-fishing has wrought havoc in some areas*. **Wrought** is an archaic past tense of **work** and is not, as is sometimes assumed, a past tense of **wreak**. There is therefore no justification for the view, sometimes expressed, that **wreaked** is an incorrect form.

ye

The history of the use of **ye** is complex. In the earliest period of English it was used only as the plural subjective form. In the

13th century it came to be used in the singular, equivalent to **thou**. In the 15th century, when **you** had become the dominant subjective form, **ye** came to be used as an objective singular and plural (equivalent to **thee** and **you**). Various uses survive in modern dialects.

your

Note the difference between the possessive **your** (as in *what is your name?)* and the contraction **you're**, meaning 'you are' (as in *you're looking well*). Note also that neither **your** nor **yours** should be written with an apostrophe.

yourself

There are two ways of using **yourself** to which nobody will object, and one which some people will criticize. The innocuous uses are:

1 to refer to the person you are speaking to: *did you hurt yourself? help yourself to some cake, Tim.*

2 to emphasize the word **you**: *you are going to have to do it yourself; did you do it yourself?*

Staff who deal with the public, in businesses such as restaurants, call centres, and the like, quite often use **yourself** in a rather different way, as a substitute for **you**: *is this soup for yourself? is the appliance for yourself, sir*? Using **yourself** in this way should be avoided in any kind of formal writing, and is considered wrong by some people even in speech. Arguably, however, it fulfils a useful function in the situations mentioned. **Yourself** sounds more formal and less direct than **you**, and is thus intended to be more polite.